WHERE THERE IS A WILL, THERE IS A WAY

ESTATE PLANNING MADE EASY FOR YOU

BY

MARCHELL G. SHORT

Where There Is A Will, There Is A Way
Estate Planning Made Easy For You

FIRST EDITION: 2024
Published by The Mothership Imprint LLC
ISBN: 979-8-9913043-0-6
Library of Congress Control Number: 2025901755

This publication is designed to provide accurate and authoritative information in regard to the subject matter covered. It is sold with the understanding that neither the author nor the publisher is engaged in rendering legal, investment, accounting or other professional services. While the publisher and author have used their best efforts in preparing this book, they make no representations or warranties with respect to the accuracy or completeness of the contents of this book and specifically disclaim any implied warranties of merchantability or fitness for a particular purpose. No warranty may be created or extended by sales representatives or written sales materials. The advice and strategies contained herein may not be suitable for your situation. You should consult with a legal or financial professional when appropriate. Neither the publisher nor the author shall be liable for any loss of profit or any other commercial damages, including but not limited to special, incidental, consequential, personal, or other damages.

Book Cover and Exhibit 1 Design: Jan-Maxwell Johnson
Illustration: Elijah Jones
Digital Design and Project Management: The Mothership Imprint LLC

DISCLAIMER

The information within this book is for informational purposes only and does not constitute financial or legal advice.

The author is not a financial planner or attorney and is not providing financial or legal advice.

All information (including templates, checklists, forms, and documents) available within these pages are provided without any warranty, express or implied, including as to their legal effect and completeness.

The information may be used as a guide and modified to meet your individual needs and the laws of your state. Your use of any information or forms is at your own risk.

MG Short Income Tax Services
www.mgshorttaxsvc.com

Where There is a Will, There is a Way

DEDICATION PAGE

To my dear parents, Bettie Mae and Clarence,

While you are no longer here physically, your love, wisdom, and guidance continue to inspire me daily. This book is dedicated to the memory of the incredible parents you were and the profound mark you left on my life. Your wisdom remains a constant source of strength.

Mom, your nurturing spirit and boundless love will forever be etched in my heart. Your warmth and kindness continue to guide me, and provide a beacon of compassion to lead me.

Dad, your strength, integrity, and the lessons you imparted remain a source of inspiration. Your legacy lives on in the values and work ethic you instilled in me.

Even in your absence, the love you shared with each other and with our family remains a testament to the enduring power of love. I dedicate this book to you both, with gratitude and love that will never fade.

In loving memory,

Marchell

TABLE OF CONTENT

Reviews

"Where There Is A Will, There Is A Way has so much information in it that everyone needs to purchase one. NOW!!!!!!"

-Linda Weaver

"Where There Is A Will, There Is A Way (WTAW) was an excellent read and very informative! The book put a lot of things in perspective regarding preparation during life and after death that I honestly never thought of. Would highly recommend everyone to read."

-Avery Murray, Jr.

"This estate planning workbook has been transformative for my spouse and me. Its practical approach made discussing sensitive topics like guardianship and beneficiaries approachable. We appreciate the clear guidance and relatable scenarios, which allowed us to get our affairs in order. It's a must-read for anyone at any stage of life! My husband and I really appreciate it."

-Kiara Henderson

"Where There Is A Will, There Is A Way provided clear and concise information regarding a wide range of issues, from financial planning to end-of-life preparation that we, or our family and friends, will have to face at some point. I read it in its entirety in one day. I plan to go back over some of the chapters. The scenarios were so well-illustrated and gave it a nice touch. I was deeply moved by the transparency of the author, revealing first-hand experiences that she and her siblings encountered while settling the estate of their parents.... Purchase the book for yourself and those you care about."

-Phyllis T Mitchell

"***Where There Is A Will, There Is A Way***, written and compiled by Marchell G. Short, is about how to make "estate planning easy."

If you do not know what to do or where to start, ***Where There Is A Will, There Is A Way***, is highly recommended. It is easy to read and has various scenarios to follow along for clarity. When my dear Mother passed away suddenly, we were all in shock, and did not have her final wishes in place. Due to not having this valuable resource, we had to learn what to do quick and fast. Talk about overwhelming and stressful. There was so much to know, do and understand, in such a short period of time.

Since receiving a copy of this book, I have begun to put things in place for myself and for other family members to avoid some of the painful lessons that we had to learn on the spot. The author has done an excellent job of simplifying terms while educating us about the necessary documents such as: legal documents, financial documents, and other documents along with passwords, and codes that we will need to have in place.

This book is truly a blessing! It is a valuable and life-changing investment, and is worth more than the selling price. Therefore, if you are considering whether to purchase a copy for yourself or your family member(s), then allow me to validate that this book is for you!"

-Deborah Greenlee

ACKNOWLEDGMENTS

Where There Is A Will, There Is A Way came about from my own personal experience back in 2012. My father, *Clarence Gordon*, had me sit down as he prepared me to be able to handle his affairs when he could not. I sat down and he had me create a list of important contacts and his final wishes. We covered details such as a funeral home director and where he would like to be buried, his insurance agent, and banker, and how to handle the details of his estate. Once I compiled the information for him it created a **One-Page Will** of sorts. Thanks, dad. Thanks for the idea of the **One-Page Will**.

There are so many other people without whom I could not have written this book. . . finished it! I want to give a special thanks to all who assisted me in bringing this book to fruition. Thank you to all who made the publishing of this book possible. THANK YOU!

Thank you to my Writing Coach, *Vivian Bell*, who always believed in me and the need for such a book. Vivian, thanks for praying for me every week, helping me through writer's block, and keeping me on track during the first year of this process.

Arletta Wilson, thanks for being with me through the initial outline, layout and organization of the book, as well as being my sounding board.

Thank you to my dear friend, *Dr. Winona Oliver*, for being the very first person to read through the entire book from cover to cover. Dr. Oliver took her Winter break to print, read, edit, and provide constructive criticism of my book, word for word. Thank You.

Thanks a million to *Robin Short*, my daughter. Thanks for believing in me. Thanks for keeping me on track whenever I seemed to slow down, stop working on the book or even felt like giving up altogether. Whenever I started to lose focus or stopped writing, Robin would quietly get me back on track. Sometimes, she would sit across from me and just begin asking me questions about where I was in my writing process and what I needed to do to get back on track; all while she was making an organized list of what I needed to do to begin writing again. Her gentle nudge helped me reschedule and reserve a study room at the Dunedin Library to get back to writing. Thanks, Robin for not letting me give up.

Thanks to *Jan-Maxwell Johnson*, Graphic Designer, who created and designed the book cover and illustrated a picture that is included in the workbook and ebook version of ***Where There Is A Will, There Is A Way***.

Thanks to *Elijah Jones*, Graphic Design student at Great Oaks High School for designing the illustration. And thanks to *George Deas, Sr.*, Elijah Jones' teacher, for connecting me with his student who was able to capture the concept.

Thanks to my publishers, *The Mothership Imprint - Jessica Rios* and *Ileah Green*; your assistance with editing, promoting the book and your gentle reminders that this book is needed, and it will help so many people be able to unlock their legacy through estate planning. Thank you.

A heartfelt thank you to several of my friends, *Kathyrn Arinsmier, Marilyn Beeler, Sacara King, Dr. Winona Oliver, Gabrielle Reese, Harrison Welch* and my sister, *Denise Gordon* who were Beta readers. Thank You.

Thanks to my cousins, *Antonio Brooks* of abrooksphotography.com and *Gregory Johnson, Jr.* of gregoryjohnsonstudios.com for taking the headshots to use in the book and for promoting the book on social media.

Thanks to my youngest sister, *Crystal Gordon*, who is my big sister. Thanks for always believing in me and reminding me that there isn't anything I can't do. Thanks, big sister.

Thanks to my long-time friend, *Linda Weaver*, who purchased the very first copy of the book when it was in the rough draft phase. Thanks, Linda for believing in me.

I want to thank my *Lord* and *Savior* for giving me the courage and faith to start with the idea of the **One-Page Will** and expand that idea into a helpful workbook for others to use. My hope and prayer is that this book reaches the people who need it the most.

Finally, to my husband of 49+ years, *Howard*, ***Where There Is A Will, There Is A Way***, wouldn't exist if you hadn't said, "Marchell, go ahead and write that book!" That's you, though. My best friend and loudest cheerleader. Down through the years, you have always believed and invested in me and made sure all my hopes and dreams come true. No matter how large or unique my dreams seemed, you have always made sure every dream I have had has come true. Howard, I dedicate this book to you; ***Where There Is A Will, There Is A Way***! Thank you, your one true love, Marchell. I love you!

Image ideation by Mr. Howard Short.
Digital illustration by Elijah Jones.

INTRODUCTION

It is a fact that all of us, black, white, rich, or poor, eventually have an unexpected or, in some cases, an expected appointment with death. Death is one of the most difficult occurrences in our lives to accept and to handle, because of the pain and grief associated with the loss of a loved one. The loss of a loved one not only impacts our life but also the lives of each person impacted by your loved one.

At the time of my father's death, since my mother was diagnosed with dementia and was incapable of handling our family affairs, I became the new matriarch of my family. Not long after the sudden and painful loss of my father, my mother passed. This new role as one of the assigned executors of their estate required that I manage the swirling problems of power of attorney, probate court, and wills, all while grieving.

And by the way, (I'll cover this later) the power of attorney (POA) ceases upon the death of your loved one. I had no clue. I thought that having power of attorney gave one control. By 'control' I mean it gave me the power to take care of my parents' business, even after their death. It wasn't until I spoke with the funeral director that I learned that while being given POA did provide control, it was only enforced while my parents were alive. Upon their death, all my POA power was relinquished. The funeral Director told me that I would need a copy of their will to conduct business on their behalf.

I am the eldest of four sisters, a brother, and several nieces and nephews who were all hurting from our loss, and they didn't know what to do or how to move forward beyond contacting the funeral director. I had to step into the role I had long dreaded and deal with the most heartbreaking events anyone could ever have to deal with - how to move on with settling my parents' estate. I had to set aside my own grief and sorrow and do what had to be done; that was to figure things out now that both our parents were deceased. My family and friends were all looking to me for answers, "What do we do now that both our parents are dead?" What are we going to do? What do we do now? What's the first thing to do?"

Their estate included two cars, the family home of 50 plus years, insurance policies, investments, bank accounts, credit card debt, monthly bills and subscriptions, numerous passwords, a Will and Trust, etc. Thank goodness there was a Will.

Being the parents of seven children, they had had the forethought to meet with an attorney and put in place a Will and Trust, naming myself and one of my other siblings, Carolyn, as executors.

My parent's forethought to plan put me in a good place as one of the assigned executors. They even thought about that: who to assign as executor of their estate. I shared the responsibility with Carolyn. In the event, that I would not be able to carry out their wishes, she would become the executor.

Having all the necessary documents in one big Estate Planning binder gave us a great sense of comfort. I wasn't starting from scratch and I wasn't starting from a place of confusion. Sure, there were lots of questions, but having their Estate Planning binder gave me a place to begin.

<u>Here's an example of how you can begin collecting the necessary information</u>

1. Personal Information

- Full legal name
- Date of birth
- Social Security number
- Contact information (address, phone number, email)

2. **Financial Information**
   - Bank accounts (checking, savings)
   - Investment accounts (stocks, bonds, mutual funds)
   - Retirement accounts (401(k), IRA)
   - Social Security benefits
   - Life insurance policies
   - Real estate properties (homes, land)
   - Vehicles (make, model, year, VIN)
   - Outstanding debts (mortgages, loans, credit cards)

3. **Legal Documents**
   - Will
   - Trust documents
   - Power of attorney
   - Health care proxy/advance directives
   - Marriage/divorce certificates
   - Birth certificates
   - Social Security card

4. **Professional Contacts**
   - Attorney (name, contact information)
   - Accountant (name, contact information)
   - Financial advisor (name, contact information)
   - Insurance agent (name, contact information)

5. **Digital Assets**
   - Online accounts (email, social media, online banking)
   - Usernames and passwords
   - Digital files (photos, documents)
   - Monthly Bills and Subscriptions:
   - Utility bills (electricity, water, gas)
   - Internet and cable providers
   - Insurance premiums
   - Subscriptions (magazines, streaming services)

6. **Other Relevant Information**
   - Safe deposit box details
   - List of valuable assets (jewelry, art, collectibles)

- Outstanding legal issues or lawsuits

Where There Is A Will, There Is A Way came about from my own personal experience. Back in 2012, my father, Clarence, had me sit down as he prepared me to be able to handle his affairs when he would no longer be able to.

Clarence said, "Marchell, write this information down."

As I sat down at my computer, he had me create a list of important contacts, along with his final wishes. We covered details such as a funeral home director and where he and my mom would like to be buried, his attorney, insurance agents (life, car, and home), banker, and how to handle the details of his estate. He even told me who to give his most cherished asset, a gold watch he had received from his older brother, Charles. That gold watch was to be handed down to his only living son, Jonathan.

At that time, I had no idea just how helpful that information would become to me and how I would be able to use it to settle my parent's estate. Once I compiled the information for my dad, it caused me to create what I call a **One-Page Will** of sorts. I say of sorts because for my dad it was only one page, but when I later began gathering and organizing my own documents my **One-Page Will** ended up being several pages long.

"Thanks, dad. Thanks for the idea of the **One-Page Will**."

I have included in the Appendix a copy of the **One-Page Will**. This document will provide an organized step-by-step format for you to begin collecting some of the vital information you will need to have access to settle a loved one's estate or for someone to easily begin settling your estate.

As I began work on this book, I realized that there is so much more that is involved in the estate planning process. I am not an attorney. I'm a retired high school teacher who happened to be the executor of my parent's estate. I do understand what it feels like to navigate these waters. My goal is to help you navigate, step-by-step, the estate planning process by helping you begin to gather, organize, and compile the necessary information from your documents to create a will.

The process of gathering, organizing and compiling documents can seem daunting. I say that because I knew where my father kept all of his important papers. He had a green box in the bottom drawer of his Chester drawer from the earliest time I could remember. We, all Clarence's children, knew about the green box and the bottom drawer. That's where he kept the birth certificates, their marriage license, death certificates, titles to the cars, keys to the house, extra keys to everybody's apartment, old Elementary School report cards, his and my mom's Social Security cards and the big Estate Planning binder; the list goes on and on. I'm laughing, "How in the world did all those documents fit into that green box?" It looked like your typical fish tackle box or an ordinary toolbox about 12" long by 6" wide and 6" in height with an internal shelf. And in truth, it tackled a lot of our problems. All of the important documents when needed throughout our childhood were in the green box.

The green box has a sentimental value, but, of course, I'm not still using the green box. I've moved with the times and am proud to say I use all the modern technology available to me. My point is to emphasize the value of having a place for your important documents along with someone, other than yourself, knowing where and how to access those documents.

It is critical to gather and organize all of your documents in an easy-to-find location. This is what I hope to help you to be able to accomplish with this workbook. I want you to be able to read through this book and find answers to many of your concerns and questions. Then, begin compiling your information to take to an attorney/lawyer to write a will or create a document to implement your last will and testament upon your death.

This workbook can be used by all ages. It's not written just for old people. This book is written with YOU in mind. ***Where There Is A Will, There Is A Way***.

THE GREEN BOX

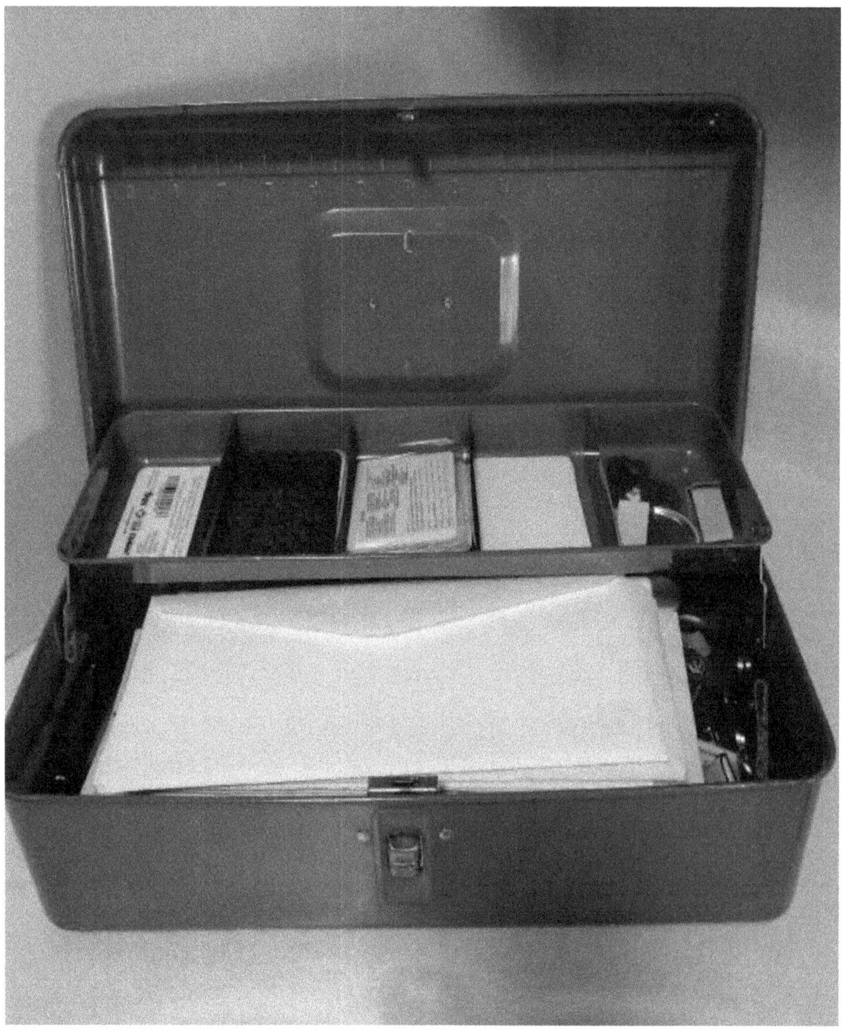

CHAPTER 1
LIFE INSURANCE

Life insurance is mainly used to replace income to your family in the event of your death. The three main types of life insurance are Term, Whole Life and Universal Life insurance.

- **Term Life Insurance**: A Term Life insurance policy is a policy that covers a specific term or amount of time (10, 20, or 30 years), and if you pass away during the term of the policy, the policy pays your beneficiaries a death benefit of a certain amount. The policyholder will expect to pay a monthly or yearly premium, with the premium increasing as the person ages. When the Term ends, the policyholder may have the option to extend the policy or convert the policy into a different type of insurance. Term Life Insurance does not have any investment value and can not be traded in sooner.

- **Whole Life Insurance**: A Whole Life insurance policy is also referred to as permanent life insurance. The policy coverage is meant to last until death and have an investment value, if the policyholder pays the premiums the policy will provide a death benefit. The premiums go toward the guaranteed death benefit and an investment account. The investment part can build over time including a guaranteed rate of return. You may borrow from the account. However, like retirement accounts, the investment part of the policy builds tax-free until withdrawals. Any value withdrawn greater than the policy will be taxed. One thing about Whole Life insurance is that it can be expensive compared to other policies, mainly due to its lifelong death benefit guarantee.

- **Universal Life Insurance**: Universal Life insurance is similar to Whole Life insurance in that the policy coverage lasts for the life of the insured, has flexible premiums, and death benefits, and has an investment value. The insured keeps coverage, as long as they pay their premiums, and the policy has a tax-deferred investment part. You can also borrow against the account. However, Universal Life insurance does not have a guaranteed return for the investment account, set premiums, or maybe even death benefit. Given the lack of guaranteed return and potential increased premiums, the policies come with more risk.

Lastly, I have seen many families whose futures were jeopardized because of the failure of not having life insurance coverage at the time of the death of the family's breadwinner. Please remember most importantly that no matter whether you and your family choose Term, Whole Life, or Universal Life insurance, the most important point is that you have insurance.

To better help you decide which type of life insurance will provide your family with the necessary coverage, please check with your local insurance providers. After you decide on what type of insurance best fits your family, pay attention to the details of your policy, and keep your beneficiaries updated as life happens.

CHAPTER 2
GUARDIANSHIP

Guardianship is a topic that should be discussed by all parents of young children and/or adult children with special needs. A discussion is warranted whether you are a single parent, married, or even divorced.

I know this can be a lot to think about. Parent(s), who would you select or designate to act on your behalf to care for young children or your adult child with special needs - if you are unable or deceased?

A guardian is an individual or individuals for whom a judge or a will gives the legal responsibility to care for a child (ward) or an adult (ward) who cannot take care of themselves. At this point, you get to decide who you think would be the best person, or persons, to raise your children, if you are unable or deceased. You can identify a family member or close friend who shares similar values and parenting philosophies as you.

The appointed individual is often responsible for both the care of the ward (the child or an adult with mental or physical disabilities) and that person's financial affairs. However, the person who shares your similar values and parenting philosophies might not be the best person to handle the finances, therefore, you can select a different guardian to handle their finances.

Once you make your decision for who will be your children's guardian, know that guardians are governed by state and local laws and serve as the ward's fiduciary. The second role - managing their financial affairs - is usually called a conservatorship in law. Remember, a guardian may be both a guardian and a conservator.

Having a discussion early on when your children are young will provide ease in the event something should happen and you are unable to care for your young children or adult child with special needs. What you don't want to do is ignore this discussion and leave your children without adequate guardianship.

I shared early on in the introduction that I am a retired Special Education teacher. In that field, I have had to have difficult discussions with parents of special needs students regarding their child's well-being even after high school. It was challenging for me as the teacher, but even more challenging for the parents to think past their child's time in school.

Eventually, the parents I worked with had to face the facts and realize that arranging care for their special needs child was important to ensure their overall well-being, safety, and quality of life in the event they would no longer be able to care for them. They had to acknowledge the fact that their child would require additional support, ongoing care, financial support, and guidance throughout their life, as well as accommodations due to physical, intellectual, and/or developmental disabilities.

It's going to take careful thought, consideration, and legal expertise when arranging care for your child with special needs. But who is better than you? As a parent, you can make the necessary arrangements for the care of your special needs child, in your will or trust. You can establish a Special Needs Trust. Please consult with an attorney experienced in special needs planning to make sure that your arrangements are legally sound and align with the laws of your state. They will be able to guide you through the process.

Once you take these steps of meeting with an attorney, you can help provide peace of mind, support, and financial security for your children even after you're no longer able to care for them.

KEY TAKEAWAYS

- Single, married or divorced parents can designate through the courts or their will and/or trust a guardian to care for their children in the event of their death or other circumstances.
- A guardian is an individual who has been given the legal responsibility to care for a child (ward) or an adult (ward) who does not have the capacity for self-care.
- A guardian may also be called a conservator when their role includes managing the finances of the child or adult who does not have the capacity to care for themselves.
- Guardians are governed by state and local laws and serve as the ward's fiduciary.
- Guardians are subject to the courts and can be asked to prepare financial statements documenting how they are managing the ward's finances.

SCENARIO: GUARDIANSHIP

Have you ever thought about who you would select or designate to act on your behalf – if you are unable?

Juan and Emma are a loving couple with two adorable children, Noah (10) and Lily (8) years old. One evening, as they sit down to discuss their long-term plans, the topic of guardianship for their children comes up. They realize the importance of deciding who would take care of Lily and Noah in the event that they are unable to do so.

Juan and Emma start by identifying family members and close friends who share their values and parenting philosophies. After careful consideration, they narrow down their choices to Emma's sister, Rachel, and Juan's best friend, Mike. Understanding the gravity of this decision, Juan and Emma decide to have a series of conversations with Rachel and Mike.

They discuss their parenting styles, expectations for the children's upbringing, and the values that are important to them. The couple wants to ensure that their chosen guardians not only have a deep affection for Lily and Noah but also align with their principles regarding education, discipline, and overall care.

After these heart-to-heart discussions, Juan and Emma feel confident that Rachel and Mike are willing to step into the role of guardians if the need arises. To formalize their decision, they decide to consult with an attorney to create a comprehensive estate plan. This plan includes a legally binding Will that clearly outlines Rachel and Mike as the chosen guardians for Lily and Noah.

In the Will, Juan and Emma also specify their wishes regarding the children's education, religious upbringing and other important considerations.

Additionally, they designate a financial guardian who will manage the children's inheritance until they reach a certain age, ensuring that their financial well-being is taken care of.

While the topic is emotionally charged, Juan and Emma find solace in the fact that they have taken the necessary steps to provide stability and love for Lily and Noah, even if unforeseen circumstances were to arise. Through open communication, thoughtful decision-making, and legal documentation, they have secured a plan for their children's future well-being.

GUARDIANSHIP FOR PETS

I don't have a pet but I have friends who have 'fur babies' and love them more than life. Absolutely, I know up close, pets are cherished members of many families, and it's important to consider their well-being and care in your estate planning, as well.

I have witnessed up close and personal the relationship some people have with their pets. My dear friend, Lidia, says she has had a pet ever since she was three years old. She lost her loving, Nove' of 10 years, last summer and could hardly wait to rescue another poodle. She rescues poodles and has dedicated her retirement years to the well-being of neglected poodles, making sure they are loved and cared for. I'm glad to say she has a new fur baby, London.

Just as we want our human loved ones cared for, it's important to designate responsible and caring individuals as guardians for our pets. This would include financial provisions, and discussing your wishes with potential caregivers, to ensure that your furry companions receive the love and care they deserve in your absence and that their needs are properly met.

SCENARIO: PET GUARDIANSHIP

Imagine a quiet gathering of two, little old ladies sitting on Lidia's comfy couch, sipping our morning coffee and watching the morning news. You know me, I bring up the topic of estate planning.

Marchell: "You know, people need to talk about their furry family members in their plans too!"

Lidia nods enthusiastically. "Absolutely! Our pets bring so much joy to our lives. We should make sure they're well taken care of if anything happens to us."

Marchell: "Exactly! So, if you're not around, who do you think would be the perfect companion for your beloved London?"

Lidia: "Well, I know my neighbor Gloria has always adored our dog, London. She lights up whenever she sees her. She'd provide a loving and caring home."

Marchell adds, "And what about our friends, Larry and Steve? They have a soft spot for animals. They're always eager to pet-sit whenever you're away. I'm sure they would embrace your furry friend like their own."

Lidia: "That's true! Larry and Steve would be fantastic choices. They'd shower my pet with love, endless belly rubs, and maybe even spoil her with extra treats."

Marchell grins. "And we can't forget to include instructions on their favorite toys, feeding routines, and any unique habits they have. After all, we want their new caregivers to understand your pet's quirks."

Lidia chuckles. "I should also make sure to leave a little something in my estate to help with her care, like providing for annual check-ups and those gourmet dog treats London loves so much!"

We share a laugh, picturing her pet living her best lives with the designated caretakers.

Remember to consult with the chosen caregivers and make the necessary legal arrangements, such as including pet provisions in your will to ensure that your pets' needs are properly addressed.

CHAPTER 3
FIDUCIARY

The term "Fiduciary" was briefly mentioned in the chapter on Guardianship as it related to guardians. "Guardians are governed by state and local laws and serve as the ward's fiduciary." A fiduciary is a relationship where one person owes another person a duty to act in the other person's interest. For example, a parent dies and in their will or trust selects a close friend to care for their child (ward) after their death. The person who cares for the child is that child's fiduciary.

One might ask, is a fiduciary only related to guardianship or is a fiduciary the same as an executor? A fiduciary may also be a person or institution you choose to entrust with the management of your property, as well. Included among fiduciaries are executors and trustees.

In the case discussed above, being a fiduciary requires being bound both legally and ethically to act in the other's best interests. A fiduciary's role often involves managing and safeguarding the assets, finances and affairs of another person, known as the beneficiary.

Fiduciary relationships are built on trust, and the fiduciary is expected to exercise loyalty, care, and diligence in fulfilling their responsibilities. They are legally obligated to prioritize the interests, avoid conflicts of interest and act in a manner that is transparent and accountable.

<u>Common examples of fiduciaries include</u>

Trustees: A trustee is appointed in your Trust to manage and administer on behalf of the beneficiaries. They have a legal duty to manage the assets of the Trust and distribute them according to the terms of the Trust.

Executors: An executor is named in a person's Will and is responsible for carrying out the wishes outlined in the Will after the person's death. The executor is responsible for handling the probate process, managing the deceased person's assets, paying debts, and distributeing the estate to the beneficiaries.

Guardians: A guardian is appointed to take care of and make sound decisions for a minor or an incapacitated adult who cannot care for themselves. The guardian is responsible for the well-being, financial management, and legal decision-making on behalf of the individual.

Agents under a Power of Attorney: An agent appointed under a power of attorney (POA) has the authority to make financial and legal decisions on behalf of another person, known as the principal. The agent under a Power of Attorney must act in the best interest of the principal and follow any and all specific instructions in the power of attorney document.

Remember, fiduciary relationships are built on trust and legal obligations. Take proactive steps such as seeking professional guidance, asking questions, doing your research, and choosing wisely, so that you can safeguard your financial interests and have peace of mind. I'll state it again; consult with legal and financial professionals for proper guidance on specific fiduciary responsibilities and requirements in your state.

SCENARIO: FIDUCIARY

Meet Yvonne, an elderly woman who has recently appointed her niece, Erika, as her financial power of attorney. Erika now acts as Yvonne's fiduciary, responsible for managing her aunt's financial affairs.

One day, Yvonne and Erika sit down together to discuss Yvonne's financial goals and plans for the future.

Yvonne: "Erika, I truly appreciate you taking on the role of my fiduciary. I trust you completely to handle my finances with care."

Erika: "Thank you, Aunt Yvonne. It means a lot to me that you have placed this level of trust in me. I promise to act in your best interests and make informed decisions."

Yvonne: "I know you will. One of my main goals is to ensure that I have enough savings to cover any future healthcare needs. I want to be prepared for any unforeseen circumstances."

Erika: "Absolutely, Aunt Yvonne. I will review your current financial situation and work with you to create a budget that allows for savings and covers your necessary expenses. We'll also explore insurance options to protect your health and your assets."

Yvonne: "That sounds great, Erika. I also want to make sure that my assets are preserved for my beneficiaries. It's important to me that my loved ones are taken care of when I'm no longer here."

Erika: "I completely understand, Aunt Yvonne. I will maintain accurate records of your assets and work with your legal professionals to ensure your wishes are reflected in your estate planning documents. We will review and update your Will and any Trusts, when necessary."

Yvonne: "Thank you, Erika. I feel relieved knowing that you're taking care of these matters. You've always been responsible and trustworthy."

Erika: "It's my honor, Aunt Yvonne. I'm committed to acting in your best interests and upholding my fiduciary duties. We'll work together to make sure your financial future is secure."

In this scenario, Erika demonstrates her commitment to acting as a fiduciary by engaging in open and honest communication with her aunt, understanding her goals and concerns, and assuring Yvonne that she will act in her best interests. They discuss Yvonne's financial goals and the steps Erika will take to ensure proper financial management, healthcare planning, and estate planning.

Effective communication and a strong bond of trust between a fiduciary and the person they represent are crucial elements in fulfilling fiduciary duties and ensuring the well-being and financial security of the beneficiary.

CHAPTER 4

WHO NEEDS A LIVING WILL AND WHY?

An advanced directive is defined as a legal document that takes effect if one cannot make decisions due to illness or incapacity. There are different types of advance directives. Some, like a living will give instructions on which measures can be used to prolong life. Others simply name a surrogate decision-maker for medical questions. And note that, different jurisdictions will generally have their own laws regarding different advanced directives.

A living will is a type of advanced healthcare directive or healthcare declaration. It is a legal document that outlines an individual's preferences for medical treatment and end-of-life care if they become unable to communicate or make decisions for themselves. It specifically addresses healthcare decisions and interventions when a person is in a terminal condition, persistent vegetative state, or an irreversible state of unconsciousness without reasonable expectation of recovery.

The question of who needs a living will and why can be answered in the following ways:

Autonomy and Personal Choice: A living will allows individuals to express their own healthcare wishes and ensure that those preferences are respected. It empowers individuals to have control over their medical treatment and end-of-life decisions, even if they are unable to communicate them in real time.

Medical Treatment Preferences: A living will enables individuals to specify their preferences regarding medical interventions such as resuscitation, life support, artificial nutrition and hydration, pain management, and other specific treatments. It ensures that family and medical professionals are aware of their choices and can follow them accordingly.

Relieving Burden on Loved Ones: Having a living will can ease the burden on family members and loved ones who may otherwise have to make difficult medical decisions on behalf of an incapacitated individual. It provides clarity, guidance, and alleviates potential conflicts and uncertainties among family members during emotional and challenging times.

Ensuring Healthcare Decisions Align with Personal Values: A living will allows individuals to ensure that their healthcare decisions align with their personal values, beliefs, religious, and cultural considerations. It provides an opportunity to express preferences based on one's own ethical and moral perspectives.

Supporting Healthcare Providers: A living will can serve as a helpful reference for medical staff and healthcare providers, enabling them to understand and respect an individual's healthcare preferences. It can facilitate communication and collaboration between healthcare professionals, patients, and their families, ultimately improving the quality of care.

While the need for A Living Will may vary based on individual circumstances and preferences, it is particularly relevant for individuals who wish to have control over their medical treatment decisions. It ensures their wishes are respected, and reduces the burden on their loved ones.

A Living Will is especially valuable for those with chronic illnesses, terminal conditions, or specific concerns about end-of-life care.

How would health care staff be able to obtain the Living Will if/when you go to the ER you are not able to tell them and your Power of Attorney (POA) is not present?

If you cannot speak for yourself and have not assigned someone medical Power of Attorney, your health care providers will look to your emergency contact(s) of your family or close friends to help make decisions about your care. If they are unsure or cannot agree, a court-appointed guardian may be requested to make the decisions for you.

It's important to consult with legal and healthcare professionals to understand the specific legal requirements and guidelines for creating a living will in your local jurisdiction. They can provide guidance on how to properly draft and execute this important document in accordance with applicable local and state laws.

SCENARIO: LIVING WILL AND/OR HEALTHCARE DIRECTIVE

Meet Steve, a college-age student who is preparing to leave for university. Before heading off to campus, Steve and his parents, Mariah and Mark, decide to have a conversation about creating a living will and healthcare directive.

> **Mariah**: "Steve, as you embark on this new chapter of your life, we want to make sure you have A Living Will in place. It's important to express your healthcare preferences, especially in case you're incapacitated and unable to communicate them."
>
> **Steve**: "I've heard about living wills, but I didn't realize it was something I should consider at my age. Why is it important?"
>
> **Mark**: "Well, even though you're young and healthy, unexpected medical emergencies happen. A Living Will ensures that your wishes are respected regarding medical treatment, especially during emergencies or if you're unable to make decisions for yourself."

Mariah: "Exactly, Steve. This is about empowering you to have a voice in your own healthcare. By documenting your preferences, you provide clarity to medical professionals and to us, your parents, in case we need to advocate on your behalf."

Steve: "That makes sense. So, what kind of decisions should I make in my living will?"

Mark: "Think about emergency situations where there might be a need for life support, resuscitation, artificial nutrition, and hydration. Consider your views on pain management, organ donation, and any specific religious or cultural considerations you want healthcare providers to know."

Mariah: "Also, think about appointing a healthcare proxy or power of attorney, someone you trust to make medical decisions on your behalf if you're unable to. This person should understand your values and preferences."

Steve: "I think I understand. It's about having a say in my own care and ensuring my wishes are respected. I appreciate you bringing this up, Mom and Dad."

Mark: "We just want you to be prepared, Steve. It gives us peace of mind too, knowing your desires are known and will be followed."

Mariah: "Let's schedule an appointment with an attorney who specializes in healthcare directives. They can guide us through the process and help you draft a living will that reflects your preferences."

In this scenario, Steve, a college-age student, learns about the importance of having a living will and healthcare directive. The conversation with his parents highlights the significance of expressing healthcare preferences and ensuring that his wishes are respected, even at a young age.

Together, they recognize the value of preparing for unexpected medical situations and decide to seek professional guidance to create a comprehensive living will that aligns with Steve's values and beliefs.

A person who is 18 years old or older, and of sound mind, can create a Living Will. Creating a Living Will means you need to choose a party you trust to carry out medical wishes on your behalf. This is called a healthcare proxy and could be a family member, a trusted friend, or an attorney.

Everyone should have a Living Will once they graduate high school and go out on their own. Living Wills can and should be updated as we age, and circumstances and wishes change in our lives.

My father had a living will healthcare directive, but he had not designated anyone as his Power of Attorney (POA). As I promised earlier in the introduction, I will explain Power of Attorney (POA). When my father became ill, was hospitalized, and later diagnosed with stage four lung cancer, he stated that he wanted me to have POA.

I immediately met with someone from the hospital's Chaplin Office. They provided the necessary paperwork that would allow my father to designate me as his POA. Like many people, I thought for sure I had the power I needed to handle his business from then on out. I did not. Power of Attorney is only valid until the person dies. Let's look at what having the Power of Attorney (POA) entails.

Chapter 5

POWER OF ATTORNEY (POA)

A Power of Attorney (POA) is a notarized, legal document that gives a designated person the power or authority to make decisions or act on behalf of another person in healthcare, financial, and legal matters if the person is incapacitated or not able to make decisions on their own behalf. Within a Power of Attorney legal document, if you are the one granting authority to a representative, you are called the principal. The representative you appoint is called the attorney-in-fact (also known as the agent depending on your state).

Power of attorney (POA) gives the designated person or attorney-in-fact the authority to act on your behalf if you are incapacitated or mentally incapable of making decisions. The person you designate can be a family member, close friend, or an attorney, and they may be given broad or limited authority to make decisions about your property, finances, real estate, investments, medical care, and more.

Types of Powers of Attorney (POA)

- **General power of attorney**: General Power of Attorney provides broad powers to the agent, allowing them to handle a wide range of financial and legal matters on behalf of the principal. It is typically used when the principal wants the agent to have comprehensive authority, such as managing their finances, making healthcare decisions, or handling their affairs. It is only valid as long as the principal is alive and competent to make decisions for him or herself and will end automatically when the principal becomes mentally incapacitated or dies.

- **Limited power of attorney**: In this case, the principal gives the agent specific powers for a particular purpose or within a particular time frame. For example, a limited power of attorney may be granted for a real estate transaction such as just to sell a specific house, where the agent can sign documents and complete the sale on the principal's behalf.

- **Durable power of attorney**: A durable power of attorney remains in effect even if the principal becomes incapacitated or mentally incapable of making decisions. This type of POA is often to ensure continuity of decision-making and care in case of future incapacity but it ends automatically when the principal dies or is revoked. This is one reason that it is very important to have a will and select an executor to carry out your wishes upon your death.

Who should have a Power of Attorney form?

Although many different situations can prompt a person to create a Power of Attorney document, Power of Attorney are used to allow someone to act on your behalf when you are not available or capable of acting for yourself.

You might want to think about making a POA if:

- You travel out of the country often.
- You work in a hazardous work environment.
- You are diagnosed with a severe illness.
- You have a business or property that needs maintenance when you're unavailable.
- You have children who would need to be provided for if you were to become incapacitated.
- You want a specific person to be responsible for your affairs.
- You want a specific person to uphold your rules about how you run your business, property, or life.
- You are approaching old age and would like to designate a representative for yourself.

A Power of Attorney is critical to have in the event of unforeseen events or circumstances, and it is often a key document of one's Estate Plan. For example, if you suddenly become ill or are involved in a serious accident, having a Durable Power of Attorney in place will allow your attorney-in-fact or agent to manage your affairs until you are better.

Consulting with an attorney experienced in estate planning or elderly care can provide you guidance on creating a power of attorney tailored to meet your individual needs and legal requirements.

CHAPTER 6

WILLS, TRUSTS, ESTATE LAWYERS, AND ATTORNEYS

Estate Lawyers and Attorneys

Before we discuss wills and trusts, we will explore the professionals who put them into place. Estate planning lawyers and attorneys are legal professionals who specialize in the area of law known as estate planning and sometimes referred to as elder law. They specialize in the interpretation of laws and the planning of the transfer of property from one individual to someone else in the event of their death or incapacitation. They provide guidance and assistance to individuals and families in matters related to the creation, administration, and distribution of assets and properties after death.

Estate planning lawyers and attorneys are trained and licensed to assist with wills. Along with drafting the legal documents they assist clients with keeping their wills and trusts updated to ensure that their intentions are clearly stated and legally binding. They also assist with the execution and probate of wills.

Estate planning lawyers and attorneys assist with power of attorney (giving a person legal decision-making ability for another), contested wills, will validity, probate proceedings, estate execution, transference, and inheritance.

Estate planning lawyers and attorneys are trained and licensed to assist with trusts. Trust lawyers advise clients on the various types of trusts available, such as revocable living trusts, irrevocable trusts, and special needs trusts. They assist in creating and administering trusts, ensuring that assets are protected and distributed according to the grantor's wishes.

Last Will and Testament: The term "last will and testament" is used interchangeably with the term "will". A will is a legal document or video that expresses an individual's wishes. It provides specific instructions about what to do with their assets. It will indicate whether the deceased leaves them to another person, or a group, or wishes to donate them to charity.

Trust: A trust is a legal arrangement in which a person (the grantor or settlor) transfers assets to a trustee to hold and manage for the benefit of designated beneficiaries.

Something to think about

What happens if you don't have a will or an estate plan in place?

- If you pass away without a will or estate plan, your assets will be distributed according to the laws of your state, which may not align with your wishes. The court will appoint an administrator, and the process may be more time-consuming and costly.

What happens to my assets if I pass away without a will and have no surviving relatives?

- If you pass away without a will or any surviving relatives, your assets may be turned over to the state. To prevent this, it's essential to create an estate plan no matter how simple, designate beneficiaries, or name charitable organizations to inherit your assets..

Wills, Trusts, and estate lawyers and attorneys play a crucial role in assisting individuals and families with estate planning needs, providing expert advice, and helping to ensure that assets are managed, and distributed according to your wishes to secure your legacy.

Take Action for Your Future

If you already have a will then all you need to do is keep it updated as life events happen. Now, if you have not taken the first step, it's time now to reach out to a qualified estate planning lawyer to discuss your unique situation. This will allow you the opportunity to create your will/trust so that your family is provided for when you are no longer here to provide for them.

I'm sure you have seen the will and trust commercials on TV or Social Media. It is true that some states may allow you to write your own will and have it notarized. Review the laws of your state to make yourself familiar with their estate planning laws. Most states require you to have your will written by a trained and licensed lawyer or estate planning attorney.

Every attorney has their own process for collecting your information. In the meantime, there are examples of worksheets in Appendix C of this workbook to help you begin gathering the necessary documents and information to create a will. For all the tech-savvy readers, we will provide electronic access to the worksheets as well.

We hope you will use this book as a guide to begin your estate planning process. Go ahead, and get started planning your estate today. Your family will be glad that you did.

Scenario 1: Choosing Between a Will and a Trust

Background

Cassandra, a 45 year old business owner, is contemplating estate planning options. She has significant assets, including a successful business, real estate, and investments. Cassandra has two teenage children from a previous marriage, and she wants to ensure their financial security. She's trying to decide between creating a Will or establishing a Trust.

Scenario

Cassandra meets with her estate planning attorney to discuss her options. The attorney explains that a Will is a legal document that outlines how Cassandra's assets should be distributed after her death. While it's a straightforward option, it may be subject to probate, a potentially lengthy and public process.

On the other hand, the attorney introduces Cassandra to the concept of a Trust. A Trust allows her to transfer assets to a legal entity, managed by a trustee (which can be herself initially), for the benefit of her children. This approach can potentially bypass probate, offering privacy and a quicker distribution of assets.

After careful consideration, Cassandra opts for a revocable living trust. This allows her to retain control over her assets during her lifetime while providing a seamless transition to her children upon her passing. The trust also includes provision for the management of her business, ensuring its continuity.

SCENARIO 2: THE JOHNSON FAMILY'S DILEMMA WILL VS. TRUST

Background

Meet the Johnsons, a family of four living in a suburban neighborhood. Maxwell, the patriarch, and Jenifer the matriarch, are successful professionals with substantial assets, including a home, savings, and investments. They have two children, Emily, 25 and Jake, 22, who are just starting their careers.

Scenario

Maxwell and Jenifer are aware of the importance of estate planning and want to ensure their assets are distributed according to their wishes. However, they are unsure whether a Will or a Trust is the right option for their family.

Factors to Consider

Minor Children: Emily and Jake are adults, but they are not yet established in their careers. Maxwell and Jenifer are concerned about their financial well-being if something were to happen to both parents.

Privacy and Probate: Maxwell and Jenifer value their privacy and want to minimize the involvement of the court. They have heard that probate can be a time-consuming and public process with a Will.

Flexibility and Control: They want to maintain control over their assets during their lifetimes but also want a plan in place for various scenarios, including incapacity or disability.

Ease of Setup: Maxwell and Jenifer are busy professionals and want a solution that is relatively straightforward to set up and maintain.

The Dilemma

The couple is torn between drafting a traditional Will or establishing a Living Trust. They see the benefits of a Will, such as its simplicity and lower upfront costs. Still, they are concerned about the potential delays and public nature of the probate process.

On the other hand, a Living Trust seems to offer more control, privacy, and flexibility. However, they are uncertain about the initial complexity of setting up a Trust and wonder if it is the right fit for their family's situation.

Resolution

Maxwell and Jenifer decide to consult with an estate attorney to get personalized advice. The attorney explains that a living trust could provide the flexibility and control they desire, allowing them to manage their assets during their lifetimes while ensuring a smooth transition in case of incapacity or death. The trust would also bypass probate, maintaining their family's privacy.

While a Will is simpler to set up, the attorney educates them on its limitations, especially in terms of privacy and control over assets.

After careful consideration and understanding the benefits of a Living Trust, Maxwell and Jenifer decide to establish a comprehensive Living Trust to address their unique family dynamics and financial goals.

SCENARIO 3: COMPREHENSIVE ESTATE PLANNING WITH BOTH WILL AND TRUST

Background

Patrick and Annie, a married couple in their early 60's have accumulated wealth throughout their lives. They own multiple properties, have diverse investments, and want to leave a legacy for their children and grandchildren. Both are concerned about potential incapacity and the seamless transfer of their assets.

Scenario

Patrick and Annie consult with an estate planning professional to create a comprehensive plan. The attorney recommends a combination of a Will and a Trust to address different aspects of their estate.

The couple decides to draft a Will that outlines their wishes regarding the distribution of personal property and appoints a guardian for their minor grandchildren. The will also designates an executor to oversee the probate process.

Simultaneously, they establish a Revocable Living Trust to hold their significant assets. By placing their assets in the trust, Patrick and Annie can avoid probate for these items, providing a quicker and more private transfer to their heirs. The trust also includes provisions for managing their wealth in case of incapacity and ensures a smooth transition of their business interests.

With both documents in place, Patrick and Annie feel confident that their estate will be well-managed. Their wishes are honored and their loved ones provided for in the most efficient manner possible.

Chapter 7
PROBATE COURT

In most situations, having a Will and Last Testament direct the disposition of your assets, such as bank balances, property, or prized possessions, will help prevent your loved ones from going to or being stuck in probate court. It will detail who is to receive property and in what amount. It can establish guardian arrangements for surviving dependents.

> **Probate**: The legal process of settling the estate of a deceased person and, more specifically, distributing the decedent's probate property to the rightful heirs.

A **probate court** is a court that has limited jurisdiction to deal with matters surrounding a person's death. Probate courts are governed by state and local laws. Some states refer to their probate courts as surrogate courts or orphan's courts because they are responsible for overseeing guardians or conservators.

Probate courts determine if testamentary documents are valid and are responsible for appointing executors to carry out the distribution plan in the documents. In some states or jurisdictions, the probate court process can be timely.

Probate courts oversee the distribution of decedent's assets according to their will or other testamentary documents. The probate court determines the distribution of the decedent's assets/property if a person dies intestate (without a Will); based on the law of its jurisdiction.

Lastly, sometimes documents are contested and in those matters, the probate court is responsible for determining if a will is authentic or not and they decide who is to receive the deceased person's property. Once it is decided, the probate court will oversee the process of distributing the deceased's assets to the proper beneficiaries.

KEY TAKEAWAYS: PROBATE COURT

Limited Jurisdiction: Probate courts are governed by state and local laws. In some areas, probate courts handle a range of matters, including guardianship, wills, trusts, and mental health issues.

Intestate Cases: The probate court determines the distribution of the decedent's assets/property if a person dies intestate (without a Will); based on the law of its jurisdiction.

Contested Matters: In contested cases, probate courts examine the authenticity of wills and decide who should inherit the deceased person's property. They also have the authority to compel executors to account for their actions if beneficiaries suspect mismanagement..

Probate Court Functions: Probate courts rule over matters related to the distribution of a deceased person's assets. They verify the validity of Wills, enforce the provisions of valid Wills, and prevent misconduct by executors and estate administrators.

Understanding the role and functions of probate courts is essential when planning your estate. Taking time to plan, including the creation of a valid Will and/or Trust and discussing matters with your family or potential executor, can help to streamline the process and ensure that your assets are distributed according to your wishes, while potentially avoiding your family months, and sometimes years, in unnecessary court proceedings.

CHAPTER 8
BENEFICIARY

A **beneficiary** is a person or group that receives money or property from someone who has died. They may receive payments from a pension plan, insurance policy, bank account, trust, etc. (Cambridge Dictionary 2024). It is important to designate beneficiaries for your financial assets so that they can be distributed according to your wishes when you pass away.

Types Of Beneficiaries

Primary Beneficiary: A primary beneficiary is an individual or organization who is first-in-line to receive benefits in a Will, Trust, retirement account, life insurance policy, or annuity upon the account or Trust holder's death. An individual can name multiple primary beneficiaries and stipulate how distributions would be allocated (Investiopedia.com, Adam Hayes, June 27, 2020).

Contingent Beneficiary: A contingent beneficiary is the designated recipient of an inheritance only if the person named as the primary beneficiary has died, cannot be located, or refuses the inheritance when the estate is settled.

A contingent beneficiary, in addition to a primary beneficiary, may be specified in a will, an insurance contract, a bank account, or a retirement account (Investopedia.com, Julia Kagan, July 31, 2024). For example, a married couple may name either spouse as their primary beneficiary and name their children as their contingent beneficiaries upon both parents' deaths.

If the primary beneficiary should predecease the owner (who wrote the will or held the policy), all proceeds can automatically go to any named contingent beneficiary.

By naming beneficiaries, you control what happens to your money and clarify the matter for all who may be involved. As stated earlier, you can name more than one primary beneficiary and more than one contingent beneficiary---you're not limited to one of each. You can set percentages for each, citing what portion of the account they should receive.

The persons who you name as beneficiary must be legally able to accept the asset in the event of your death. Having beneficiaries simplifies the settling of your estate and can reduce potential stress for those you leave behind.

Beneficiaries designated for financial accounts such as an insurance policy, bank account, or retirement accounts aren't usually affected by changes to a will. These direct designations take precedence.

FAQ: What is the significance of naming beneficiaries on financial accounts, and what happens if I don't have anyone named as a beneficiary?

- It is important to name beneficiaries on your financial accounts in order to designate who will receive your account assets, upon your death. Naming beneficiaries can help delay distributions and potentially help avoid the probate process.
- If the deceased did not name a beneficiary or write a will, it gets more complicated, and the probate court would have to name an executor to manage the distribution of the money after any debts are paid. Probate can be timely and costly.

Remember, failure to name beneficiaries in a will or on financial accounts can result in the financial institution holding the assets and making decisions about the distribution of your assets, which can tie up one's property in probate for months and, in some states, years. It can leave decisions about how to distribute your assets up to the state in which you live. In either case, the people you want to provide financial support after your death may not receive it or they may have to wait a long time for it.

You can change the beneficiary on any financial account at any time, although doing so requires completing and returning the relevant paperwork to the institution.

It might be useful to know if you are the beneficiary of a life insurance policy, that while the principal of most policies is not taxed the accrued interest might be. See your tax professional to discuss your specific details. The names of beneficiaries in financial account documents may remain private, however, a will becomes a public record and can expose heirs to public scrutiny.

Additional Types of Beneficiaries

Payable On Death (POD): "Payable on death" is a designation used for certain financial accounts, such as bank accounts, certificates of deposit (CDs), and retirement accounts like IRAs (Individual Retirement Accounts). When an account owner designates a beneficiary as "payable on death," it means that upon the account owner's death, the assets or funds in that account will be automatically transferred to the named beneficiary without going through probate. This process is relatively simple and usually requires the beneficiary to provide a death certificate and identification to claim the assets (Investopedia.com, Julia Kagan, June 2024).

A Payable On Death (POD) account is more powerful than a last will and testament. If a POD account has one individual named as the beneficiary, and the will of the account holder lists another individual as a beneficiary, the POD-designated beneficiary prevails. The named beneficiary on the POD account is not required to honor the account holder's last will and testament, which makes it imperative that the individual ensures to change or cancel the POD beneficiary if they have someone else listed on their will (Investopedia.com, Julia Kagan, June 2024).

- Transfer-On-Death (TOD): Transfer-on-death automatically transfers property, like vehicles, and securities (stocks, bonds, mutual funds, or brokerage accounts) to a designated beneficiary upon the death of the person who owned the property, without probate. A beneficiary may be an individual or an organization, such as a charity. The beneficiary does not have access to the property until the death of the owner (Cornell Law School, September 2021).

It's advisable to consult with your financial institution or service provider regarding payable on transfer and transfer-on-death (TOD) to better understand the options available to you in your state or jurisdiction to ensure that your assets are appropriately designated to align with your estate planning goals.

TAKE ACTION: CHOOSE A BENEFICIARY.

Naming a beneficiary is completely up to you. Who will be the best choice for my beneficiary or beneficiaries? Below is a list of questions to consider when thinking of who to name as your beneficiary or beneficiaries; this method may help you order and narrow down your beneficiary list. Think about the following:

- Does anyone depend on you financially?
- Are you married?
- Do you have children?
- Do you have a favorite charity or cause?

All these factors could come into play when you're deciding who will benefit from your estate as a beneficiary.

SCENARIO: IMPORTANCE OF UPDATING BENEFICIARIES

As your life changes, first job, new job, address changes, marriage, children, divorce, become a single parent, relocate etc. you will need to update your information. Keeping your information up to date is critical. Updating your information might be something that you do once a year at the beginning or end of the year or on your birthday. It is good to look at your circumstances and update your will every five years or so. Emphasis on the need to review and keep your documents up to date.

Real-life example: It was 2020. After listening to several podcasts, because that was all we had time to do. Remember? It was evident that many young people had their mom as their beneficiary on paperwork at their very first job right out of college. One such man, who suffered an untimely Covid-death, was married but had never updated his beneficiary to include his new spouse and children. His mother received his death benefit, instead of his spouse and children. The mother, wrapped in grief, felt that her son loved her and meant to leave the inheritance to her, instead of his spouse and children.

I shared this example to try to emphasize the importance of updating your information as you age and as your life circumstances change.

SCENARIO: PRIMARY AND CONTINGENT BENEFICIARIES OF A MIDDLE-AGED WOMAN

Meet Dena, a middle-aged woman who is reviewing her estate plan with her attorney, Crystal. They are discussing the selection of primary and contingent beneficiaries for Dena's assets.

Dena: "Crystal, I'm updating my estate plan, and I want to make sure I have my beneficiaries clearly designated. Can you explain the difference between primary and contingent beneficiaries?"

Crystal: "Certainly, Dena. Primary beneficiaries are the individuals or entities who will receive your assets directly upon your passing. They have the first claim to your estate. Contingent beneficiaries, on the other hand, are the backup beneficiaries who will inherit your assets if the primary beneficiaries are unable to do so."

Dena: "That makes sense. So, for my primary beneficiaries, I want to ensure my children receive equal shares of my estate. They are my top priority."

Crystal: "Great! We can list your children as primary beneficiaries and specify the percentage or specific assets they will receive. Now, let's discuss contingent beneficiaries. Who would you like to designate if, for some reason, your children are unable to inherit your assets?"

Dena: "I think it would be wise to name my siblings as contingent beneficiaries. They have always been there for me, and I trust them to handle my estate if my children are unable to do so."

Crystal: "That sounds like a good choice, Dena. It's important to have backup beneficiaries in case the primary beneficiaries are unable to receive the assets. By naming your siblings as contingent beneficiaries, you have a solid plan in place."

Dena: "Thank you, Crystal. I feel relieved knowing that my estate plan includes both primary and contingent beneficiaries. It gives me peace of mind that my assets will be distributed according to my wishes, no matter the circumstances."

Crystal: "You're welcome, Dena. It's essential to review and update your beneficiary designations periodically, especially after major life events like births, deaths, or changes in relationships. That way, your estate plan remains current and aligned with your intentions."

Dena: "I will definitely keep that in mind. Thank you for your guidance, Crystal."

In this scenario, Dena consults her attorney, Crystal, to ensure that her primary and contingent beneficiaries are clearly designated in her estate plan. They discuss Dena's intentions and preferences, resulting in a plan where Dena's children are the primary beneficiaries, and her siblings serve as contingent beneficiaries. By considering different scenarios and having backup beneficiaries in place, Dena ensures that her assets will be distributed according to her wishes, providing her with peace of mind.

SCENARIO: PRIMARY AND CONTINGENT BENEFICIARIES WHEN YOU ARE SINGLE WITH NO CHILDREN

Meet Curtis, a single individual who is working with his estate planning attorney, Robin, to determine primary and contingent beneficiaries for his assets.

Curtis: "Robin, I'm in the process of creating my estate plan, but I'm unsure about selecting primary and contingent beneficiaries. I don't have a spouse or children. What are my options?"

Robin: "Good question, Curtis. Since you don't have a spouse or children, you have more flexibility in choosing beneficiaries. Let's explore some possibilities together."

Curtis: "I have a close relationship with my sister, Gabrielle. She has always been there for me. Could I name her as the primary beneficiary?"

Robin: "Absolutely, Curtis. You can designate your sister, Gabrielle, as the primary beneficiary. She will directly receive your assets upon your passing. It's important to discuss your intentions with her to ensure she is comfortable with this responsibility."

Curtis: "That makes sense. And what if, for some reason, my sister is unable to inherit my assets? Who could be the contingent beneficiary?"

Robin: "In that case, you have several options. You could consider other close family members, such as your parents, nieces, or nephews. Additionally, you may choose to name a charitable organization or a cause you feel strongly about as the contingent beneficiary."

Curtis: "I see. Since I have a close relationship with my parents and they have supported me throughout my life, I think I'll name them as the contingent beneficiaries. If anything happens to my sister, I want my assets to go to them."

Robin: "That sounds like a thoughtful decision, Curtis. By designating your parents as contingent beneficiaries, you have a plan in place to ensure your assets go to loved ones in case your sister is unable to receive them."

Curtis: "Thank you, Robin. I feel more confident now that I have a clear understanding of primary and contingent beneficiaries and how they apply to my situation."

Robin: "You're welcome, Curtis. It's important to periodically review and update your beneficiary designations as your circumstances change. That way, your estate plan remains current and aligned with your wishes."

Curtis: "I will keep that in mind. Thank you for your guidance, Robin."

In this scenario, Curtis, a single individual without a spouse or children, consults his attorney, Robin, to determine primary and contingent beneficiaries for his assets. He decided to designate his sister as the primary beneficiary and his parents as contingent beneficiaries. By selecting close family members, Curtis ensures his assets will go to loved ones in the event his primary beneficiary is unable to inherit. This thoughtful planning provides Curtis with reassurance that his estate plan reflects his intentions.

CHAPTER 9
SOCIAL SECURITY

In recent news, there have been reports of adult children continuing to receive Social Security benefits intended for their deceased parents for an extended period of time, even years after the parent's death.

SCENARIO: NIGHTLY NEWS - JANUARY 2023

In a United States District Court, a woman admitted to cashing more than $128,000 of her deceased mother's Social Security benefits. According to the court documents, she collected her mother's monthly benefits for several years after her mother's death, before she was caught by the Social Security Administration. After the Social Security Administration launched an investigation, she was found and pleaded guilty.

> *"Concealing a relative's death from the Government in order to keep receiving the relative's Social Security benefits constitutes felony theft."*

Social Security Payment

The Social Security Administration was founded on August 14, 1935, with the passing of The Social Security Act, during the Franklin Roosevelt administration. The Social Security Administration was created to protect the elderly and to provide a safety net for workers and their families.

We know that the Social Security Administration provides a source of income and services for eligible Americans, such as retirement, disability, Medicare, and Supplemental Security Income SSI. Parents can apply for Social Security benefits for their special needs child. You can access the website https://www.ssa.gov/ssi/text-child-ussi.htm for more information.

The Social Security benefit is a monthly check that replaces part of your income when you reduce your hours or stop working altogether once you reach the age of 62 - 70 years old or for special needs children as early as birth. A monthly Social Security benefit depends on factors such as your income, living situation, things you own, and whether you are disabled or a widow(er).

Retirement benefits for surviving spouses

You might ask, "What does Social Security have to do with estate planning?"

For many Americans, Social Security benefits are a vital part of their monthly budget. If your spouse precedes you in death it is good to know that you may qualify, if you're the spouse, divorced spouse, child, family member, or dependent parent of someone who worked and paid Social Security taxes before they died, to continue receiving benefits (https://www.ssa.gov/survivor).

As a surviving spouse or the executor for a deceased person who received Social Security benefits, it is imperative to report the person's death immediately to the Social Security Administration. Social Security can't pay benefits for the month of death. That means if the person died in July, the check received in August, (which is payment for July) must be returned. If the payment is by direct deposit, notify the financial institutions as soon as possible so they can return any payments received after death.

For many Americans, Social Security is not enough to replace their working income to pay for their monthly expenses as they age. That's why it is necessary to plan ahead for your retirement.

TAKE ACTION

The rules for receiving Social Security benefits are complex and vary depending on your situation. If you haven't talked with one of the Social Security representatives about retirement benefits, or if yourcircumstances have changed, contact your local Social Security office to discuss the choices available to you.

- Social Security Administration: 1(800) 772-1213; TTY 1(800) 325-0778
- Hours 8:00 a.m. - 7:00 p.m. Monday through Friday

CHAPTER 10

ASSETS: PERSONAL AND REAL PROPERTY

This book is written for all ages and I am sure there are many readers on both ends of the spectrum - either acquiring assets or starting to eliminate assets. Where are you? Are you busy acquiring and accumulating assets or are you at the place in life where you are starting to eliminate and downsize as many personal assets as possible?

- **Assets**: Assets are often defined as something having value, such as possession of property, that is owned by a person, business, or organization. Assets range from real property like real estate to personal property like vehicles, jewelry, cash, bank accounts, retirement accounts, and digital assets. (Cambridge Dictionary 2024).

Assets can easily be classified into categories of personal and real property.

- **Personal Property:** Personal property is a type of property that includes any tangible and or intangible asset of value that can be owned by a person and is distinct from real property. Personal property is movable; that is, it isn't fixed permanently to one particular location.

  Personal property can be characterized as either tangible or intangible. Examples of tangible property owned by an individual, such as home appliances, clothing, vehicles, jewelry, boats, and furniture. These assets tend to depreciate in value over time.

Other kinds, such as artwork, antiques, and collectibles which can be included in a will or trust may appreciate in value. Stocks, bonds, and bank accounts are a few examples of intangible personal property that can also be included in a Will or Trust.

- **Real Property:** Real Property is immovable assets, assets such as a parcel of land and anything permanently attached to it, buildings, or natural resources. These are fixed assets that cannot be easily moved or altered. Real property can be classified as residential, commercial, agricultural, industrial, or special purpose.

Real estate may include your family residence, vacation home, timeshare, or vacant lot. The owner of real property has the rights of ownership, including the right to possess, sell, lease, and enjoy the land as well as pass it on through a will, trust, or other estate planning.

KEY TAKEAWAY: UNDERSTANDING PERSONAL PROPERTY VS. REAL PROPERTY

Personal Property

Movable Assets: Personal property consists of movable assets that are not permanently fixed to one place.

Depreciation and Appreciation: Some personal property, like appliances and clothing, typically depreciate in value over time. Other properties like artworks and antiques may appreciate in value.

Tangible and Intangible: Personal property can be categorized as tangible (appliances, vehicles) or intangible (stocks, bonds, bank accounts).

Real Property

Permanent Attachment: Real property includes a parcel of land and all structures and assets permanently attached to that land.

Ownership Rights: The owner of real property has the rights of ownership, including the right to posess, sell, lease, and enjoy the land.

Classification: Real property can be classified depending on how it is used, such as residential, commercial, agricultural, industrial, or special purpose. The classification affects the rights associated with the property.

Understanding the distinction between personal property and real property is crucial for property owners, as it impacts ownership rights, legal obligations, and financial considerations, including the potential for property appreciation or depreciation.

TAKE ACTION

Family Discussion: Communicate your wishes with your family members. Open discussions can help prevent disputes over who gets certain items of personal and/or real property.

Inventory Your Assets: Create a list of your personal and real property including both tangible (vehicles, furniture, and collectibles) and intangible (bank accounts, stocks, and bonds) including their value, and update the list periodically.

Consult Legal and Financial Professionals: Consult estate planning attorneys and financial advisors who specialize in estate planning matters. They can help you create a plan that is unique to you and your personal and real property to ensure a smooth transition of assets..

Review and Update Your Estate Plan: Once you have met with an estate planning attorney, regularly review your estate plan, especially if there are significant changes in the value of your assets.

Consulting with professionals, and reviewing and updating your estate plan will ensure your personal and real property are managed and properly distributed according to your wishes.

CHAPTER 11
PASSWORDS FOR DIGITAL ASSETS

Passwords for digital assets are a no-brainer these days. For many of us, they are our first line of security for our online accounts. We rely on them for various purposes. Some of us have pages and pages of passwords written in a little black book, in Google, or Apple, on the notes pages on our iPhones or Androids. While others use the same password for everything. I sure hope the last example is not you.

There are many people who have passwords that date back to the times before the year 2000 (commonly known as Y2K). For those of you who are unfamiliar with that term, I encourage you to Google Y2K to understand its significance in computer history.

We all know that just because we have passwords that date back a while, we should be diligent with making sure that our passwords whether they are for work, home, or our entertainment, are updated, changed periodically, and securely stored.

You might ask, "How might I securely store my passwords?"

"I don't use the same password for everything, no, that's not me."

"Well, I use Google, Microsoft, or Apple to store my passwords."

Or you might even say, "I only use strong passwords that aren't easy to decode."

As for securing your passwords, you should consider a method that is convenient for you and one that balances accessibility and safety. You should have someone in mind (spouse, close friend, or whoever you have designated as the executor of your estate) that you can entrust with access to your passwords in the event you become incapacitated or in the event of your death.

Key Takeaway

- You use passwords on a daily basis and should protect your digital assets and passwords securely.
- The individual you designate as the executor of your estate can also be the person you entrust with access to your passwords.
- Decide the method that works best for you to store your passwords whether they are in a physical notebook, password manager app, notes section of your smartphone, etc.
- Whatever method you choose, remember to communicate your intentions clearly with the executor of your estate.
- Keep your digital account and password information updated as you modify or add passwords over time.

When you entrust a person with access to your passwords, in the event you become incapacitated or in the event of your death, you ensure that they can manage your accounts, computers, and phones, appropriately. Being mindful of this aspect can help you avoid complications and ensure a smooth transition of your digital presence after you're no longer here.

TAKE ACTION

I'll leave you with something to think about. Who should you grant access to your passwords, and what measures can you adopt to ensure their security effectively?

CHAPTER 12
TAXES

"Death and taxes" is a phrase commonly referencing a famous quotation written by American statesman Benjamin Franklin:

> Our new Constitution is now established and has an appearance that promises permanency; but in this world, nothing can be said to be certain, except death and taxes.
>
> *-Benjamin Franklin, in a letter to Jean Baptiste Le Roy, 1789*

Though Franklin is not the progenitor of the phrase, his usage is the most famous, especially in the United States (en.m.wikipedia.org).

In America, the date April 15th is, for some, the most dreaded. For many other Americans, taxes are a topic they don't quite understand, nor enjoy talking about. The old adage is true; even in the year of an individual's death, taxes still need to be accounted for and fulfilled according to federal, state, and local regulations and laws. To be able to complete a tax return or furnish essential details and information to a tax professional, it will be necessary to obtain the deceased's financial records and be able to provide a certified death certificate.

According to the IRS website, all income must be reported up to the date of death, this includes any and all claims of eligible credits and deductions. If the deceased had not filed individual income tax returns for years prior to the year of their death, you may have to file those as well. The IRS also states that it's your responsibility (the surviving spouse or the executor of the estate) to pay any balance due and to submit a claim if there's a refund.

If you are the surviving spouse or the executor of an estate, you can refer to the IRS website, Section titled "File the Final Income Tax Returns of a Deceased Person (https://www.irs.gov/individuals/file-the-final-income-tax-returns-of-a-deceased-person) for detailed information regarding how to file and prepare the final individual income tax return of a deceased person. The IRS website lists and provides several resources such as forms and publications.

KEY TAKEAWAY: FILING TAXES FOR THE FINAL YEAR

Tax responsibility: The responsibility for filing the final tax return usually falls on the surviving spouse, if there is one, the executor or personal representative of the deceased person's estate. They are responsible for gathering the necessary financial information, having the tax return prepared accurately, and paying any taxes owed or filing a claim for the refund.

Determine the filing status: Was the deceased single, head of household, married filing jointly, or qualifying widow(er)? File accordingly.

Use the appropriate tax form(s): See the IRS website for forms and publications. More importantly, consult with a tax professional for professional advice.

Report income and deductions: According to the IRS website, all income must be reported up to the date of death, as well as any and all claims of all eligible credits and deductions.

Before beginning the process, I suggest that you consult with a tax professional to seek guidance to ensure you comply with requirements when filing taxes for the deceased's final year (https://www.irs.gov/individuals/file-the-final-income-tax-returns-of-a-deceased-person).

CHAPTER 13
MONTHLY BILLS AND SUBSCRIPTIONS

As I discussed in the Introduction of this book, I was the designated executor of my parents' will, trust, and estate at the time of their death. My father was a very organized and frugal man and like most men of the early 1950s, he worked hard and took care of paying all of the bills. My mother was a stay-at-home mom until all the children were old enough to go to school.

My dad paid the household bills; all the bills except my mother's Saks Fifth Avenue credit card bill. He felt that Saks Fifth Avenue was too overpriced and didn't want to have anything to do with what my mom thought was a necessity; shopping at Saks Fifth Avenue. She was responsible for paying her own monthly Saks Fifth Avenue credit card bill; for which she proudly paid each month. It afforded her a monthly trip to Saks to pay the bill.

Looking back, I'm amazed that a lot of people's monthly subscription costs in 2024 are higher than my parent's total household bills when they were raising seven kids. At the time of my parent's death, they had only six or seven monthly bills which included Duke Energy, Spectrum, Water Works, car and house insurance, and maybe a credit card or two.

My point exactly. Just think for a moment. Especially after COVID-19, most American households have more streaming channels alone, not including their everyday bills, than my parents had combined.

I know things have changed. A lot of us pay most of our bills online or have set up automatic monthly withdrawals. That's why this chapter is so important when you are estate planning. It is crucial to inform the executor of your estate to help ensure that they have the necessary information to handle your bills and subscriptions according to your wishes after you pass away or become incapacitated and can't take care of your own monthly bills and subscriptions.

Let's think for a moment. "Who does the monthly family budget? Who knows what bills are due, when they're due, and from what account(s)? Who pays the bills?

After reading the chapter on Social Security, you learned that your Social Security is one of the benefits that stop at the time of your death or as soon as the Social Security Administration has been notified. Veteran Administration benefits are another benefit that stops as soon as a person dies. However, there are many monthly bills and subscriptions and even yearly subscriptions that will automatically continue until the company is notified of your passing. If you use an automatic withdrawal at your bank or credit union, I am sure at some point you have had a payment withdrawn that you had forgotten that you had scheduled.

"Right?"

If you are the one who handles paying the bills then you know your specific bills and subscriptions can vary depending on your family's circumstances and preferences. Note: If you are reading this chapter and have no idea how the bills in your family are paid, please ask the person who pays the bills to explain the process to you. It will benefit you to be informed.

In some households, the wife pays certain bills and the husband pays the rest of the bills. To better ensure that the executor of your estate handles your bills and subscriptions according to your wishes, it will be good to include service provider, contact information, account names, numbers, due dates, and if they are being automatically withdrawn from which account(s) as well.

TAKE ACTIONS

- Compile a comprehensive list of your monthly, and yearly bills and subscriptions.
- Include details such as the name of the service provider, account numbers, contact information, and any relevant login credentials (passwords).
- Share (communicate with your executor) the location of the list and any important documents; by providing physical copies, storing them in a safe deposit box and sharing the key, or using digital methods like passwords, or providing access to an online password manager.
- Regularly review and update the list of bills and subscriptions to ensure it remains accurate. If you add or cancel services, be sure to inform the executor to ensure your list remains as accurate as possible.

To ensure your wishes are carried out properly, clearly communicate your expectations and make sure the executor understands their role in managing these matters in the event you become incapacitated or pass away.

If you are not comfortable with sharing your list, you can always consult with an attorney to ensure that your wishes are appropriately documented. An attorney could incorporate specific instructions in the will or trust to help guide the executor.

CHAPTER 14

OTHER RELEVANT INFORMATION

Just like we discussed in the last chapter on Monthly Bills and Subscription, it is important to include a comprehensive list of your valuable assets in your will. Now, of course, this list will vary depending on your family circumstances and preferences.

Assets are something having value, such as possession of property, that is owned by a person, business, or organization. Assets range from real property like real estate to personal property like vehicles, jewelry, cash, collectibles, antiques, furniture, bank accounts, retirement accounts, and digital assets (Cambridge Dictionary 2024).

Below are some common types of assets that people often include as part of their estate plan.

Real estate: Properties like houses, land, or commercial buildings that you own.

Financial accounts: Bank / Credit union accounts, savings accounts, certificates of deposits (CD), and investment accounts like stocks, bonds, and mutual funds.

Retirement accounts: Individual retirement accounts, IRA, 401(k) plans, pensions or any other retirement savings accounts.

Life insurance policies: Any life insurance policies (term, whole life, universal life, etc.) that you hold, specifying the beneficiaries who will receive the payouts.

Personal belongings: Valuable items like jewelry, artwork, antiques, collectibles, furniture, and other possessions you wish to distribute to specific individuals. Cars, motorcycles, boats, or any other motor vehicles you own are also considered personal belongings.

Business interests: If you have a business or have shares in another company, it is a good idea to create an Exit Plan to specify how you want your ownership interest to be handled.

Digital assets: Explain how you want your online accounts, email accounts, social media profiles, and any other digital assets with value or sentimental significance to be handled.

Debts owed to you: If someone owes you money, you can specify how these debts can be handled or forgiven in your will.

Trusts: It is important to mention that you have a Trust in your will and specify and outline just how the assets held in the trust should be distributed.

When beginning your estate planning, it is a good idea to consult with an attorney who specializes in estate planning to ensure that you tailor your will to reflect your specific assets and wishes.

CHAPTER 15
COMMON ESTATE PLANNING MISTAKES

Many topics regarding estate planning have been covered throughout this workbook and to avoid making mistakes it will help you to be reminded of some of the possible common estate planning mistakes.

Flashback: "Is estate planning just for the rich and famous or just the elderly? Who needs an estate plan?"

Estate planning is beneficial for all people, even younger individuals or those with modest assets, who often assume that estate planning is only necessary for the wealthy or elderly. Consequently, one of the most common estate planning mistakes is failing to have a comprehensive estate plan in place. Everyone should have an estate plan, regardless of your financial status.

Estate planning is a critical aspect of your financial security, ensuring that your assets are distributed according to your wishes after your passing. Unfortunately, many people make common mistakes that can lead to unintended consequences. Remember, everyone should have an estate plan, regardless of their financial status.

KEY TAKEAWAYS: COMMON MISTAKES TO AVOID IN ESTATE PLANNING

1. **Procrastination**: Delaying action. Many people put off estate planning

thinking that they have plenty of time. We all know that things can happen at any time, making it necessary to plan ahead. Sometimes people just don't want to deal with the topic of death and dying at all.

2. Neglecting to have a Living Will and Power of Attorney: *Healthcare and financial decisions*. A living will is a written, legal document that lets your doctor and family know the treatments you would and would not want to be used to keep you alive, as well as our preferences for other medical decisions such as end-of-life pain management or organ donation. (Mayo Foundation for Medical Education and Research, August 2, 2022). Power of Attorney (POA) is a notarized legal document that gives a designated person the power or authority to make decisions or act on behalf of you in healthcare matters, and financial and legal matters if you are incapacitated or dead.

3. Failing to update your Estate Plan: *Life Changes*. As your life changes, so should your estate plan. Significant events such as marriage, divorce, the birth of children, the death of a spouse, or as you acquire assets, it becomes necessary to update your will, trusts, and other estate planning documents.

4. Neglecting or Overlooking Beneficiary Designations: *Asset Ownership*. Beneficiary designations on retirement accounts, life insurance policies, and other assets like bank accounts can override your will. Be sure these designations align with your overall estate plan. If you fail to designate beneficiaries or keep them up to date on your financial accounts and other assets, it can lead to unintended consequences, such as your assets going to the wrong individuals or being subject to probate unnecessarily.

5. Not considering taxes: *Estate taxes.* Depending on the value of your estate and the state you live in, certain laws might apply to your assets after you pass. Proper planning can help minimize or eliminate these taxes. See your tax professional.

6. DIY Estate Planning: *Complexities.* You can write your own estate plan with online templates, however, they may not address all your potential scenarios. Consulting with an estate planning attorney can ensure your plan is comprehensive and legally sound.

7. Failing to Consider Probate: *Court process.* Probate can be a lengthy and costly process. Trusts can help avoid probate, but they may not be suitable for everyone. Consulting with an estate planning attorney can ensure your plan is comprehensive and legally sound.

8. Forgetting About Digital Assets: *Online accounts.* As referenced in Chapter 10: Passwords for Digital Assets, it's important to consider your online accounts, such as your social media profiles, email accounts, digital files, cryptocurrencies, and online banking to name a few. Forgetting to address these assets in your estate plan can lead to complications and difficulties for your loved ones in accessing or managing them. Designate a digital executor to manage these accounts.

9. Not Communicating Your Wishes: Keeping your estate plan a secret. Keeping your estate plan a secret from your family or beneficiaries can cause a lot of confusion and bad feelings after you pass. It's important to communicate wishes as openly as possible with your loved ones and explain why you've made certain decisions.

TAKE ACTION

To avoid making these common estate planning mistakes, you can begin today to collect and organize your information using the Worksheet to Complete in Appendix C. This Worksheet may also be accessed electronically.

Once you have compiled most of your information, then it is essential for you to work with an experienced estate planning attorney who is familiar with the laws of your specific state. Consulting with an estate planning attorney can ensure your plan is comprehensive and legally sound to your specific circumstances that align with your goals and objectives.

As your life changes, regularly review and update your estate plan to protect your assets and ensure your wishes are carried out.

CHAPTER 16
YOUR JOURNEY TOWARDS SECURE ESTATE PLANNING

In writing this workbook, my goal was to make estate planning easier to understand. I have explained the complicated parts and shown you how to make a good plan with the help of a lawyer who specializes in estate planning.

<u>The Road You've Traveled</u>

Let's reflect for a moment on the journey you've taken:

- You learned some of the basics of estate planning and why it's important for everyone, no matter how much or how little money they have.

- You explored different legal documents used in estate planning, including healthcare directives, will, trusts, powers of attorney, payable on death (POD), and transfer-on-death (TOD), to name a few.

- We talked about the important choices you need to make, like who gets your stuff, who takes care of your kids and your pets, and who manages your finances if you are incapacitated or at your death.

- You learned about special considerations for different life situations, such as being married, single, having no living relatives to leave your assets to, or if you own a business.

- We discussed common mistakes in estate planning, procrastination, outdated documents, forgotten digital assets, and family disagreements, and how to avoid them.

Your Empowered Future

As you conclude this book, remember that estate planning is not something that you do one time, but a task that should be an ongoing part of your life. And by that I mean, that as your life changes, so should your estate plan.

Regularly Review Your Plan. Life changes, and so should your estate plan. Review your plan every few years or whenever significant events occur, like marriage, divorce, births, or acquiring new assets.

Communicate Your Wishes. Communication helps avoid misunderstandings and family arguments down the road. Be sure to openly discuss your estate plan with your loved ones and/or beneficiaries.

Seek Professional Guidance. Doing estate planning on your own can be a challenge or, to some of us, an impossible feat. Consult with an experienced estate planning attorney who will assist you in creating a plan that will be unique to your circumstances and keep it compliant with current regulations.

Plan for Digital Assets. Don't forget to include your digital assets in your estate plan. Create a list of your electronic subscription payments, accounts, and passwords, or consider using a digital manager with access by the executor of your estate.

Consider Charitable Giving. Explore opportunities for leaving a legacy through charitable donations or endowments if you have no close family.

Your Legacy

With an estate plan in place, you can ensure a lifelong commitment to securing your legacy and providing for those you love and cherish. Remember that your estate plan is more than just a stack of cumbersome paperwork. It shows how much you value and care for your family, and what causes are important to you. It's your way of taking care of the future and making sure your legacy lives on.

By starting your estate plan, you've taken a big step towards peace of mind and financial security for yourself and your loved ones. You've turned a difficult task into something more manageable and empowering.

Don't forget that estate planning is not set in stone. It should change as your life changes. Keep working on your estate plan throughout your life to make sure it reflects your wishes and needs.

Thank you for choosing ***Where There Is A Will, There Is A Way*** as your guide. I wish you a future filled with prosperity, happiness, and the peace of mind that comes from knowing you've created a plan that reflects your wisdom and love.

CHAPTER 17

A.D. AFTER DEATH

We know, we know, nobody ever really wants to talk about death and dying except the undertaker; that's her or his job, and we are thankful somebody does it. This chapter will be short, brief and to the point. We promise. We just didn't want to help you get organized and plan your estate without bringing up the topic of death. Estate planning is all about planning to ensure that after your death, things run as smoothly as possible for the ones left behind.

Let's look at A.D. - After Death, from the perspective of a surviving widow or from the perspective of surviving family members, siblings, or close friends. It's a little easier talking about death if we aren't talking about our own death, we know.

In an ideal situation, we know the last wishes of the deceased (husband, father, or close friend) because they have left a well-drafted, up-to-date estate plan, have a will, and/or have a will and trust. Hopefully, they have openly discussed their final wishes with their family members, and you feel well equipped to handle their estate.

You get that call! Oh my God, that dreaded call! The call that the (husband, father, or close friend) has died. Immediately, a plethora of emotions set in. For some, it's a shock! For others, it is guilt. And still, for others, it is an overwhelming grief. Sometimes it is a crippling grief where one is barely able to catch their next breath.

Oftentimes, depending on our personalities, we take a deep breath, shift into automatic drive, and begin taking care of things; contacting close family and friends, starting the process of making funeral arrangements, looking for the legal documents (will/trust) and oftentimes catch ourselves making quick, off the top of our head, decisions about changing things.

As for our elderly parents, we might immediately start thinking about turning off the utilities in the family house, selling their car, or clearing out the house by throwing their things away, all in a mad rush to get back to our own lives, to just get it over with. Which isn't the best thing for ourselves or our grieving families.

For those of us who have been through this before, though, we know the importance of slowing down and not acting in haste. Grieve and breathe. Then give yourself some grace and know that however you are feeling and thinking things through, on any given day, it's normal to grieve some more.

It has been said that grief comes in waves. If you have ever gone to the beach or seen pictures of the ocean, they highlight the magnificent movement of the waves. Waves are unpredictable events, such as your grief. Grief is our natural response to loss. After the loss of a loved one or close friend, you might experience all the stages of grief at any given time.

Now let us briefly explore the five stages of grief written about by Swiss American psychiatrist, Elisabeth Kubler-Ross in 1969.

THE FIVE STAGES OF GRIEF

Denial: When you first learn of a loss, it's common to think, "This can't be happening to me." You may feel shocked or numb.

Anger: As reality sets in, you're faced with the pain of your loss. "Why is this happening to me? Why didn't they ______?"

Bargaining: During this stage, you dwell on what you could have done to prevent the loss. "If I had only done this or that, this wouldn't have happened. I should have ______."

Depression: Sadness sets in as you begin to understand the loss and the effect the loss has on your life. "I'm too sad to do anything."

Acceptance: In this final stage of grief, you accept the reality of your loss. "I'm at peace with what happened."

All of these stages of grief may not come in this precise order, but they will come. Because you may be bargaining first, and then full of anger. It is human instinct to act. Like throwing a buoy to a drowning man in the ocean, we want to do something to ease the pain of a loss. Grief is a deeply personal experience, and the way you handle it is unique to you.

SCENARIO

For someone who has been through this before, they'll alert you to slow down, breathe, and give yourself some grace.

Marchell: (Experienced executor) "Breathe! Just take a breath. Slow down. Don't make any quick decisions like selling the house or selling the car. You might need that car yourself in a few months. Slow down."

Sandra: (Surviving spouse) "Slow down? How can I slow down? I have all of this to take care of and I want to get it done. No, waiting is not an option."

Marchell: (Experienced executor) "Locate the legal documents like the Estate planning binder or the Worksheet you Completed: "One-PageWill" where you have everything organized."

Sandra: (Surviving spouse) "Thanks for your patience. I'm glad you're here to help me think because this is a lot. I feel like curling up in my bed and never coming out again. (Tears rolling down her face). "I miss Clinton, so much."

Marchell: (Experienced executor) "I believe you. I believe you miss Clinton. You two have been married since you were kids. You can get through this. Just know that grief comes in waves."

Sandra: (Surviving spouse) Thanks to ***Where There Is A Will, There Is A Way***, I'm using the Worksheet I completed in the back of the book as a checklist to ensure I have everything I need to begin settling the estate.

Marchell: (Experienced executor) "Great! Continue checking off each task as you complete it. But please give yourself at least six months before you make any major decisions. You don't want to do anything you'll regret six months down the road."

CHAPTER 18
YOUR LEGACY STARTS WITH A SPENDING PLAN

Testimonial: Robin E. Short

You may be thinking "I won't have anything to leave for my family except for debt." It may seem that everything is becoming more expensive, and you aren't making more money. However, that doesn't have to be your truth. With a plan, you can become aware of your financial situation and change it accordingly. In this short chapter, we will cover debt, budgeting, debt repayment, credit cards, and your *Why*.

The first step is to compile a list of current bills and debt. What may be helpful is to look at your checking account and credit card statements to see what charges have come out in the last 1-3 months. It may be helpful to use Credit Karma, which is an online personal finance company that offers free credit scores and shows open and closed accounts associated with your name. It is very informative. By showing open and closed credit card accounts, car loans, mortgage loans, student loan debt, and items in collections, you can get a detailed look at your financial situation.

There are several ways that you might have outstanding debt and be unaware: perhaps you co-signed on a purchase with someone, and they later stopped making payments, your spouse/partner bought something on a joint account, your child's medical bill or student loan or a change of address kept a bill from getting to you. Don't forget to list subscriptions that come out automatically monthly and any pending "after-pay purchases" that might be deducted for a series of weeks or months.

I'll warn you to be patient with this part, because it can be difficult to see how much money you've spent on purchases, and because depending on how many banks and credit card accounts you have, it may take some time to look through your spending history. This will be a great time to assess any repeated purchases that are adding up. List it out!

Next, evaluate your income. Sometimes our financial situation is strained because we aren't making enough money, and we may not be bringing in enough income. It can be very hard to live debt-free and contribute to our retirement fund if we are struggling with monthly bills. What you are earning versus what you are spending is an aspect to consider, and this will vary according to our financial situations so consider it as you identify where you stand financially. You may have to give yourself grace for your current situation, but also consider what changes can be made that can start to rectify your financial situation.

Budget. When you hear "budget" you may instantly think "Tuna and crackers" from now on. Rest assured that it doesn't have to be like that at all. I recently heard it referred to as a "spending plan"- hopefully you are relaxed again. In our first step, we compiled "Who You Owe" and you have a better idea of how and what you are spending your money on.

Now, let's make it visual, either paper and pencil, a basic Excel spreadsheet or there are some mobile apps you can use. Feel free to search "free budgeting apps". I keep mine very basic, I use a simple chart and list 3 categories and a bonus section.

<u>3 Categories (plus 1 Bonus Section)</u>

Who Do I Owe?
How Much Do I Owe or How Much Do I Plan to Pay this Month?
What Day of the Month Do I Owe It?

Bonus Section

Upcoming Expenses

a. This category is for expenses that are approaching this month or the next couple of months
b. Here I might list: Christmas, summer trip, my mother's birthday, oil change

There are many ways to pay off debt. Two of which I will briefly discuss; are the debt snowball or debt avalanche methods. Many people have been very successful in paying down or paying off debt using these methods. The basic idea with both is to be sure to make the minimum payment and ON-TIME payments for all outstanding debt.

But with the debt snowball, the smaller debt is tackled first then the amount that was being paid on the smaller can all be aimed at the larger debt. With the debt avalanche method, the debt is tackled by paying off accounts with the higher interest rate first. They both have the end goal of eliminating debt.

If you are trying to decide which is better for your financial situation, please take the time to research both. So far, we have compiled expenses and debt, looked at our income, and developed a spending plan, now let's pick on the thing that negatively affects many people.

Credit Cards: A Debt Pitfall

Credit cards can be sneaky. A quick swipe here. Minimum payments can be large. A quick tap there. Credit card perks seem endless, free this, free that. Yearly credit card fees can seem harmless, just $600, but don't forget those perks. Available credit card limits magically increase by $2,000 because you are such a great credit card holder allowing for more swipes and taps. I'll pay off the balance as soon as I get paid on Friday. Quick swipe here, 70% of the credit card payment went to interest. Quick tap there. My credit card maxed out. The credit card statement says if the minimum payment is made it will take 17 years to pay off the balance. What's one more credit card...it's just to get us through Christmas.

There are so many types of debt we can acquire. But I'll pick on credit cards here. As you read above, credit card debt can sneak up on you. You get it "just in case there is an emergency" and next thing you know, there has been $10,000 worth of emergencies. A fancy dinner because you were having a bad day, a quick trip to Hawaii, Super Bowl tickets, a flat tire, a new outfit, coming to a friend's financial rescue, and on and on.

This is not coming from a place of judgment, but just to show how easy it is to get into debt because life happens. This is a good point to mention an "emergency fund" or "saving for a rainy day". An emergency fund is essentially a financial cushion that can help when unexpected expenses arise.

As soon as I approached 18 years old when credit card companies started reaching out, I was warned and very aware of how credit card debt and interest works. I made a commitment to myself to never use my credit card for gas or food. My thinking was food would be a distant memory, and gas would quickly all be driven out, but guess what? Once that credit card cycle ends, you will be receiving a bill for both next month and many meals ago.

Of course, everyone's situation is different, this worked for me, but you can assess your spending and maybe you might decide for yourself specific purchases that you will not buy with your credit card. You might decide not to use your credit cards for Starbucks or when you tell your kids you can't afford something that they want and they tell you to just use your credit card, that might be a good way to discuss financial debt, discipline and the possible danger of credit cards to your children.

Your Why. So far you have gotten to think about your financial picture and maybe the work involved in becoming debt-free to be able to leave a legacy to your family. This is a great point to think about why being debt-free or even taking steps towards it is important to you. Some people have a reactive mindset or better yet say things like "things will work out" when it comes to their finances but imagine how you and your family's life can be different with a proactive mindset, a plan, and goals. Everyone's Why might look different, but I'll share some ideas you may not realize are even possible for you.

Possible ideas

- Retire and maintain a comfortable lifestyle
- Leave an inheritance to their children, siblings, or extended family members
- Cover the college tuition of the next generation of their family
- Be able to assist in a home down payment or business ownership for a family member
- Retire from their job and open a business you are passionate about
- Retire early
- Travel the world
- Put an end to going through your list of who you can borrow from this week
- Spend your time and resources for a cause you are passionate about

These are just some ideas I have seen people achieve. Maybe your ideas look different. Take some time to decide your Why and the impact that you can have not only in your own life but also in the lives of others.

What could be possible if you follow a spending plan, spend wisely, and can eliminate debt, save money, contribute to your retirement savings, and invest?

KEY TAKEAWAYS

- Compile a list of bills, expenses, and debts.
- Make a spending plan and re-visit it often.
- Keep an eye on factors affecting your credit.
- Assess what aspect of debt is your biggest challenge, examples: late

fees from late payments, car loans, credit cards, etc.
- Determine and remember your Why.

TAKE ACTION FOR YOUR FUTURE

As you improve your financial situation, find opportunities to educate the next generation about finances or those who are struggling with spending and debt.

Testimonial: Robin Short

Fuzzy. I was asked to give my experience of becoming debt-free. I had to look through emails to remember when I became debt-free because I had blocked it out of my head. "What year did I pay off my student loan?" "What year did I pay off my car loan?" It's such a blessing that this can be fuzzy in my brain, versus it being a constant nag and financial barrier or limitation.

Between the 3 items on my debt snowball: my credit card, student loan, and car loan, I had accumulated $70,000 in debt. When I started Financial Peace University in April 2015, I owed $56,058. As of 2021, I had paid all my debts off... Yes, Yay!! My strategy was to know my due dates, not miss payments, use a budget, use the debt snowball system, be intentional not to acquire more debt, and pay EXTRA.

I had always been financially conscious of the world of credit cards and debt. But, I was also reasonable that some of the things like education (college degree) and reliable transportation could move me forward in life. I was a single mother so the better I could do; the smoother things would be for my family and household. So, I did feel like I'd been practical in the debt I had acquired.

I had been making headway before I started Financial Peace University, but once I gained the knowledge of how the debt snowball works I was able to have a personal goal to "pay all my debt off." I employed a strategy to approach the complete payment of the smallest debt first, which was my credit card debt. Then, I was able to focus those resources that I had been paying on my credit card debt on my car payment. Lastly, I paid off my student loan debt.

When COVID started, the government put into place the "Suspension of Payments and Interest" for student loans. There are two ways this could have been taken: a relief or an opportunity. For me, it was an opportunity to make significant progress in paying down my student loan. I had no idea that I could potentially pay it completely off. Since they had no idea how long COVID would last, they initially made the suspension for a couple of months, and after some time, I heard the suspension was being extended. Some people would be happy because it meant no payments for them and more money in their pockets, but I was thrilled for the update because it meant my payment was all being directly applied to the principal. I was fortunate to be working during this time, so it allowed me to have the income coming in to change my future.

Based on my interest rate on the loan, I calculated when I made a payment how much was going to the principal and how much was going to interest. With this suspension of interest, all my payments, for the first time in the history of my loan, were going to the principal, and it was easier to see the progress. This motivated me and I made it a priority. If I had extra money, even as small as $10, I would use it to make a payment.

Looking back, I didn't celebrate this financial discipline and accomplishment enough. Unfortunately, I reached this accomplishment during COVID-19, so celebrating wasn't the easiest or the priority. The extent of my celebration was that I shared it with a few friends and family members and changed up a few lines on my budget paper.

Tips that I use to stay in the debt-free mindset are to use wisdom and discipline, plan for purchases, save and plan for unexpected expenses, because yes, something will ALWAYS come up. I keep very clear at the front of my mind that debt acquired MUST be paid back.

Paying off my loan allowed me to focus on some items that I felt I was behind on such as contributing to my son's college savings fund or my retirement savings. I could also use it for saving for a rainy-day fund, savings, household bills, or projects. I've tried to share the knowledge I've learned with my son.

I had a friend who was sharing what they thought was news that I would get excited about, "I just heard that they are passing a law that might give you student loan forgiveness." I looked at him and said, "I paid off my student loan two years ago." This breaking news was not applicable to me and this is a great feeling.

APPENDIX A
FREQUENTLY ASKED QUESTIONS REGARDING ESTATE PLANNING

What is estate planning?

Estate planning is the process of creating a comprehensive plan for the management and distribution of your assets and affairs, both during your lifetime and after your death. It involves making important decisions about how your property and wealth will be transferred to your chosen beneficiaries, minimizing taxes, and ensuring your healthcare and financial wishes are respected.

Do I need an estate plan even if I don't have significant assets?

Yes, absolutely. Estate planning isn't solely for the wealthy. Even if you have modest assets, an estate plan is essential. It provides guidance on asset distribution, appoints someone to make decisions on your behalf if you become incapacitated, and ensures your wishes are followed.

What documents are typically included in an estate plan?

Common documents in an estate plan include a Last Will and Testament, a Revocable Living Trust (if necessary), a Durable Power of Attorney for financial matters, a Healthcare Power of Attorney, an Advance Healthcare Directive (Living Will), and beneficiary designations for accounts like life insurance policies and retirement plans.

How would health care staff be able to obtain the Living Will when you go to the ER you are not able to tell them and your POA is not present?

If you cannot speak for yourself and have not assigned someone medical Power of Attorney (POA), your health care providers will look to your emergency contact(s) of your family or close friends to help make decisions about your care. If they are unsure or cannot agree, a court-appointed guardian may be requested to make the decisions for you.

How often should I update my estate plan?

You should review and update your estate plan whenever significant life events occur, such as marriage, divorce, birth or adoption of children, significant changes in assets, or when you want to change your beneficiaries or make other adjustments. Regular reviews, at least every few years, are advisable.

What is the difference between a will and a trust?

A will is a legal document that outlines how your assets should be distributed after your death, while a trust is a legal entity that holds and manages assets for the benefit of specific individuals or entities during your lifetime and after your death. Trusts can help avoid probate and provide more control over the distribution of assets.

What happens if I don't have a will or an estate plan in place?

If you pass away without a will or estate plan, your assets will be distributed according to the laws of your state, which may not align with your wishes. The court will appoint an administrator, and the process may be more time-consuming and costly.

How can I minimize estate taxes for my heirs?

Strategies to minimize estate taxes may include gifting, setting up trusts, and making use of the lifetime estate and gift tax exemption. Consult with an estate planning attorney for guidance tailored to your situation.

What is the role of an executor in estate planning?

An executor, named in your will, is responsible for managing your estate after your death. Their duties include gathering assets, paying debts and taxes, and distributing assets to beneficiaries as specified in your will.

How can I address digital assets and online accounts in my estate plan?

You can address digital assets by creating a list of your online accounts and specifying how they should be handled in your estate plan. Consider appointing a digital executor to manage these assets.

What should I consider when choosing guardians for my children?

When selecting guardians for your minor children, consider factors like the guardian's values, parenting style, location, financial stability, and willingness to take on the responsibility. Be sure you discuss your choice with them beforehand and consider a backup guardian as well.

If I'm single and have no living relatives, who should I choose as beneficiaries in my estate plan?

In such a situation, you have the flexibility to choose beneficiaries based on your values and philanthropic interests. Consider selecting charitable organizations, friends, or even specific causes you care about. You can leave a lasting legacy by supporting causes that matter to you.

What are some charitable giving options for me in my estate plan if I have no close family?

Leaving a charitable legacy can be deeply fulfilling. You can include charitable bequests in your will, establish a charitable trust, or name charitable organizations as beneficiaries of your retirement accounts or life insurance policies. Consult with an estate planning attorney to explore the most suitable charitable giving options for your goals.

Who should I appoint as my executor or trustee if I have no family members or close friends to fulfill these roles?

In the absence of family members or close friends, consider appointing a trusted professional, such as an attorney, accountant, or financial advisor, as the executor or trustee. Alternatively, you can designate a reputable corporate trustee, like a bank or trust company, to manage your estate and ensure your wishes are carried out impartially.

What happens to my assets if I pass away without a Will and have no surviving relatives?

If you pass away without a Will or any living relatives, your assets may escheat, which means they could be turned over to the state. To prevent this, it's essential to create an estate plan and designate beneficiaries or charitable organizations to inherit your assets.

Are there any specific considerations or legal obligations I should be aware of when I don't have a family to inherit my estate?

Without close family, it's crucial to clearly outline your wishes in your estate plan. Additionally, consult with an estate planning attorney to address any specific legal requirements in your jurisdiction. You may want to include contingency plans or consider options like creating a charitable foundation to manage your assets in perpetuity.

What are the benefits of using trusts in estate planning?

Trusts offer several benefits in estate planning, including:

- Avoiding Probate: Assets held in a trust typically avoid the probate process, which can save time and reduce costs.
- Privacy: Trusts are private documents, unlike wills, which become part of the public record after probate.
- Control: Trusts allow for detailed control over how assets are distributed, including conditions for beneficiaries.
- Flexibility: Trusts can be tailored to accommodate specific goals, such as providing for minor children, individuals with special needs, or charitable giving.
- Asset Protection: Some trusts, like irrevocable trusts, can shield assets from creditors and lawsuits.

How can I ensure my business interests are properly handled in my estate plan?

Business owners can ensure their business interests are properly addressed in their estate plan by:

- Creating a buy-sell agreement that outlines what happens to the business upon their death or disability.
- Designating a successor or successor(s) to manage and continue the business.
- Considering whether to transfer ownership through a trust or other mechanisms.

Ensuring that the value of the business is accurately assessed for estate tax purposes.

What is the significance of naming beneficiaries on financial accounts, and what happens if I don't have one?

Naming beneficiaries on financial accounts is crucial because it determines who will receive the account's assets upon your death. If you don't name a beneficiary or if the named beneficiary predeceases you, the assets may become part of your estate and go through the probate process, delaying distribution and potentially subjecting the assets to creditor claims or estate taxes.

How can I protect my estate from potential legal challenges or disputes among beneficiaries?

To minimize the risk of disputes and legal challenges, you can:

- Clearly communicate your wishes to family members and beneficiaries.
- Use a no-contest clause in your Will or Trust, which disinherits beneficiaries who challenge the document.
- Seek professional guidance to create a well-drafted and legally sound estate plan.
- Consider mediation or alternative dispute resolution methods in your estate plan.

Is estate planning affected by changes in state laws if I move or own property in different states?

Yes, estate planning can be affected by changes in state laws when you move or own property in multiple states. Each state has its own laws regarding Wills, Trusts, and Probate. It's essential to review and update your estate plan when you relocate or acquire property in a different state to ensure it aligns with the laws of your current residence and property locations. Consulting with an attorney experienced in multistate estate planning can be invaluable in these situations.

How to minimize inheritance tax?

Minimizing inheritance tax, also known as estate tax or death tax, involves careful estate planning. Here are some strategies that may help reduce the impact of inheritance tax, although it's important to note that tax laws and regulations can vary between jurisdictions, so it's advisable to consult with an attorney or tax professional who specializes in estate planning:

Lifetime gifts: Gifting assets during your lifetime can help reduce the value of your estate subject to tax. Many jurisdictions have annual and lifetime gift tax exemptions that allow you to gift a certain amount without incurring tax. By strategically gifting assets to your beneficiaries, you can transfer wealth and potentially lower the taxable estate.

Utilize tax exemptions and deductions: Familiarize yourself with the specific inheritance tax exemptions and deductions available in your jurisdiction. These can include exemptions for spouses, charitable donations, and specific types of assets. By leveraging these exemptions and deductions, you can reduce the taxable amount of your estate.

Establish trusts: Trusts can be useful for estate planning and minimizing taxes. Irrevocable trusts, such as bypass or credit shelter trusts, allow you to transfer assets out of your taxable estate while still providing for your beneficiaries. Consult with an attorney to determine the most appropriate type of trust for your situation.

Consider life insurance: Life insurance proceeds are generally tax-free for the beneficiary. By having life insurance policies that pay out to your beneficiaries, you can provide them with additional funds while potentially reducing the taxable estate.

Charitable contributions: Making charitable donations through your estate can help lower the taxable estate while supporting causes you care about.

Be sure to understand the rules and regulations related to charitable deductions in your jurisdiction.

Plan for business succession: If you own a business, a well-structured succession plan can minimize the tax impact on your estate. Transferring ownership or utilizing business succession tools like family limited partnerships or limited liability companies can help reduce the taxable value of your business assets.

Seek professional advice: Estate planning and tax laws can be complex, so it's crucial to work with an experienced attorney or tax professional who specializes in estate planning. They can provide personalized guidance based on your financial situation, goals, and applicable tax laws.

Remember that the effectiveness of these strategies may vary based on your specific circumstances and the tax laws in your jurisdiction. It's important to consult with professionals who can provide tailored advice based on your individual needs.

APPENDIX B
WORKING GLOSSARY

Adjudication: refers to the legal process of resolving a dispute or deciding a case. When a claim is brought, courts identify the rights of the parties at that moment by analyzing what were, under the law, the rights and wrongs of their actions when they occurred (Cornell Law School 2024).

Adjudication of disability: Social Security determines disability claims through a network of local SSA field offices. The application and related forms ask for a description of the claimant's (the person who is requesting disability benefits) impairment(s), treatment sources, and other information that relates to the alleged disability (www.ssa.gov, September 2024).

Assets: Assets are something having value, such as possession of property, that is owned by a person, business, or organization. Assets range from real property like real estate to personal property like vehicles, jewelry, cash, bank accounts, retirement accounts, and digital assets (Cambridge Dictionary 2024).

Beneficiary: a person or group that receives money or property from someone who has died. They may receive payments from a pension plan, insurance policy, trust, etc. (Cambridge Dictionary 2024).

Primary Beneficiary: A primary beneficiary is an individual or organization who is first-in-line to receive benefits in a Will, Trust, retirement account, life insurance policy, or annuity upon the account or trust holder's death. An individual can name multiple primary beneficiaries and stipulate how distributions would be allocated (Investiopedia.com, Adam Hayes, June 27, 2020).

Contingent Beneficiary: A contingent beneficiary is the designated recipient of an inheritance only if the person named as the primary beneficiary has died, cannot be located, or refuses the inheritance when the estate is settled. A contingent beneficiary, in addition to a primary beneficiary, may be specified in a will, an insurance contract, or a retirement account (Investopedia.com, Julia Kagan, July 31, 2024).

Conservatorship: A conservatorship is when the court appoints a conservator to manage a person's affairs, who is unable to handle them due to their mental capacity, age, or physical disability. A person who is unable to handle their financial affairs or daily life responsibilities will be considered incapacitated by the court, so the court will assign a conservator to make decisions on behalf of the person. Conservatorships are governed differently in each state depending on their laws. Please check with your state. A judge may appoint a family member as the conservator or an independent party who has no relation to the conservatee. A judge may also choose to appoint a conservator and a guardian, where the conservator handles the conservatee's financial affairs and the guardian handles the person's physical and medical care. In some cases, the conservator and guardian can be the same person.

To make sure the Conservator does not take advantage of the conservatee, they must update the court regularly on a financial accounting of the conservatee's assets. For major decisions like selling the conservatee's home, they will have to seek permission from the court before moving forward.

The conservatee's assets help to pay the Conservator and the court reviews these payments to make sure they are reasonable. The conservatee has rights and they or their relatives can ask for the conservator to be removed and replaced if the Conservator is not performing their duties. They can also have the Conservatorship removed if they feel the appointment is no longer necessary.

Also, if the conservatee dies or their assets deplete, a Conservatorship can end (Cornell Law School, November 2021).

Death Benefit: The death benefit of an insurance policy is the amount of money paid to the beneficiary (the person you choose to give the money to) when the policyholder (person insured) dies.

Digital Assets: Assets in electronic form, such as cryptocurrency, your online accounts, and digital files.

End-of-Life Plan: Instructions of one's final wishes for their medical care, and funeral arrangements, as one comes to the end of their life.

Escheat: Escheat is the passing of an interest in land to the state when a decedent has no Will, no heirs, or devisees. In the United States, escheat rights are governed by the laws of each state. Probate is usually used to determine escheat rights (Cornell Law School 2024).

Estate Lawyers: Estate lawyers are estate planning professionals who help individuals create, manage, and execute the individual's Will and Trust requests.

Estate Planning: Estate planning is the process of preparing to manage an individual's financial situation if they are incapacitated or upon their death. Planning ahead includes planning how a person wishes to have their assets distributed to their heirs or beneficiaries and how to settle their estate taxes, and debts as well. Included in the estate plan is the consideration of the guardianship of minor children and pets. Most estate plans are set up with the expert assistance of an attorney. Some of the steps include listing assets and debts, reviewing accounts, and writing a will (Investopedia.com, Julia Kagan April 22, 2024).

Executor: a designated person appointed in a Will and or Trust to carry out the wishes of the deceased, manage the estate's administration, and distribute assets to any beneficiaries.

Fiduciary: Fiduciaries are persons or organizations that act on behalf of others and are required to put the client's interests ahead of their own, with a duty to preserve good faith and trust. Fiduciaries are thus legally and ethically bound to act in the other's best interests.

A fiduciary may be responsible for the general well-being of another (e.g., a child's legal guardian), but the task usually involves finances—for example, managing the assets of another person or a group of people. Money managers, financial advisors, bankers, insurance agents, accountants, executors, board members, and corporate officers all have fiduciary responsibilities (Investopedia.com, Adam Hayes, March 19, 2024).

Gift Deed: A legal document used to transfer ownership of real or personal property from one person to another.

Guardianship: Guardianship is a legal arrangement where an individual is appointed by the court to manage or make decisions for and care for another person (ward), typically a minor child or incapacitated person. Guardianship is often used to give responsibilities of managing a child's welfare to an individual besides their parents in situations where a proper parent is not available.

Some adults may end up under guardianship (also called conservatorship for adults) when a court determines they have a disability that prevents them from taking care of themselves or they become reckless or harmful to themselves. For more information on conservatorship, see Conservatorship. Like Conservatorship, each state regulates the guardianship laws when and how they are used (Cornell Law School, January 2022).

Inheritance: Money, land, or possessions received from someone after the person has died. (Cambridge English Dictionary, 2024)

Inheritance Tax: A tax attributed by some jurisdictions on the value of an individual's inherited assets or estate, which is often paid by the beneficiary rather than the estate.

Irrevocable trust: This is the type of trust that cannot be changed or revoked by the person who created it (grantor). The grantor gives up ownership of the assets and transfers them to the Trust, which is then managed by a trustee. An irrevocable trust cannot be modified, amended, or terminated without the permission of the grantor's beneficiary, or by the order of the court (Investopedia.com, Julia Kagan, August 31, 2024).

Last Will and Testament: A legal document that designates a person's last wishes for the distribution of their assets and the appointment of a guardian for their minor children after their death.

Life Insurance: Life insurance is used to replace income to your family in the event of your death. The three main types of life insurance are term, whole life, and universal life insurance.

Living Will: A living will is a written, legal document that lets your doctor and family know the treatments you would and would not want to be used to keep you alive, as well as your preferences for other medical decisions, such as end-of-life pain management or organ donation (Mayo Foundation for Medical Education and Research, August 2, 2022).

Medical Healthcare Directive: similar in purpose to a "Living Will", advanced healthcare directives need to be in writing and each state has different forms and requirements for creating the legal documents. Your forms may need to be signed by a witness and/or notarized.

- Please check with your state.
- Keep the originals in a safe but easily accessible place.
- Give a copy to your doctor.
- Give a copy to your healthcare agent and any alternate agent.
- Talk to family members and other important people in your life
- about your advanced directives.
- Carry a wallet-size card that indicates you have a healthcare
- directive.
- Keep a copy with you when you are traveling.

(Mayo Foundation for Medical Education and Research, August 2, 2022).

Passwords: Access credentials and digital codes used to secure online accounts and assets may need to be managed or passed on in an estate plan.

Payable on Death (POD): A designation on a financial account or asset that states who will receive the proceeds or ownership of the asset upon the account holder's death.

Personal Property: A type of property that includes any tangible and or intangible asset of value that can be owned by a person and is distinct from real property. Tangible assets owned by an individual, such as vehicles, jewelry, furniture, and collectibles can be included in a Will or Trust.

Policyholder: Insurance policies have a policyholder. A policyholder is the person who purchased and owns an insurance policy as well as pays the insurance premium. Your name is on the account, and you are the only one who can change it by changing the beneficiaries or adding insured individuals.

Power of Attorney (POA): A notarized legal document that gives a designated person the power or authority to make decisions or act on behalf of another person in healthcare, financial, and legal matters if the person is incapacitated or not able to make decisions on their own behalf.

Probate: A judicial proceeding by which a testamentary document is established to be a valid Will (Cornell Law School 2024).

Probate Court: A court of limited jurisdiction that hears matters surrounding a person's death. Most frequently, probate courts oversee the distribution of the decedent's assets according to their Wills or other testamentary documents and direct the distribution of the decedent's assets if they die intestate (without a will). Probate courts are responsible for determining the validity of testamentary documents and appointing executors to carry out the distribution plan in the documents.

Some probate courts also hear petitions to declare people incompetent and oversee guardians or conservators, while other jurisdictions leave these matters to family courts.

Probate courts are governed by state and local law and they derive their power and jurisdiction from statute. In some states, probate matters are handled by probate divisions of ordinary courts. Some jurisdictions refer to their probate courts as surrogate courts or orphans' courts (Cornell Law School 2024).

Real Property: Real Property is immovable assets, assets such as land, buildings, and real estate, which can be passed on through a Will, Trust, or other estate planning.

Revocable trust and revocable living trust: A revocable trust and revocable living trust are used in estate planning. A revocable trust and a living trust are separate terms that describe the same thing. A trust can be changed at any time. The grantor or trustor makes the trust. While alive the grantor/trustee makes decisions about the money or property in the revocable living trust. A trustee can be a person or a financial institution, who will carry out the wishes of the grantor if he becomes incapacitated or upon his or her death. The people who receive the money or property from the revocable living trust are called the beneficiaries (www.consumerfinance.gov May 14, 2024).

Social Security: A government program in the United States that provides retirement (monthly compensation) for older people, people whose husbands or wives have died, and people who are unable to work because they are sick (Cambridge English Dictionary, 2024).

Tax Return - Final Tax Return After Death: The surviving spouse or executor of their estate, can file and prepare the final individual income tax return of a deceased person the same way you would if the person were alive. Report all income up to the date of death and claim all eligible credits and deductions.

If the deceased had not filed individual income tax returns for the years prior to the year of their death, you may have to file. It's the responsibility of the surviving spouse or executor to pay any balance due and to submit a claim if there's a refund (IRS.gov 2024).

Transferable on Death (TOD): Transfer-on-death automatically transfers property, like vehicles, and securities to a designated beneficiary upon the death of the person who owned the property, without probate. A beneficiary may be an individual or an organization, such as a charity. The beneficiary does not have access to the property until the death of the owner (Cornell Law School, September 2021).

Trust: A legal arrangement where one party (the trustee) holds and manages assets for the benefit of another (the beneficiary), according to the terms specified in a trust document.

APPENDIX C
WORKSHEETS

I. Sample Worksheet

Here's an example, using generic placeholder names and information to demonstrate how to begin gathering and collecting your pertinent information for your will and/or final wishes:

1. **Personal Information**
   - Full legal name: John Doe
   - Date of birth: January 1, 1960
   - Social Security number: XXX-XX-XXXX
   - Contact information: 123 Main Street, Anytown, USA, 12345
   - Phone number: (555) 123-4567
   - Email: johndoe@email.com

2. **Financial Information**
   - Bank accounts: XYZ Bank (checking), ABC Credit Union (savings)
   - Investment accounts: Brokerage Firm XYZ (stocks), Mutual Fund Company ABC (mutual funds)
   - Retirement accounts: Company 401(k), Traditional IRA
   - Life insurance policies: XYZ Life Insurance Company
   - Real estate properties: Primary residence at 456 Elm Street, Anytown, USA, 12345
   - Vehicles: 2010 Toyota Camry, VIN: XXXXXXXXXXXXXXXXX
   - Outstanding debts: Mortgage with XYZ Bank, Auto loan with ABC Credit Union, Credit card with DEF Bank

3. Legal Documents

- Will: Prepared by Attorney Jane Smith
- Trust documents: Revocable living trust
- Power of attorney: Attorney John Johnson
- Health care proxy/advance directives: Primary care physician Dr. Sarah Anderson
- Marriage/divorce certificates: Marriage certificate with Jane Doe, Divorce certificate from Mary Doe
- Birth certificates: Children's birth certificates

4. Professional Contacts

- Attorney: Jane Smith, Law Firm ABC
- Accountant: John Johnson, Accounting Firm XYZ
- Financial advisor: Michael Brown, Financial Planning Firm DEF
- Insurance agent: Sarah Wilson, Insurance Agency GHI

5. Digital Assets

- Online accounts: Email (johndoe@email.com), Social media (Facebook, Twitter), Online banking (XYZ Bank)
- Usernames and passwords: Stored in a secure password manager
- Digital files: Photos and important documents stored on a computer and external hard drive

6. Monthly Bills and Subscriptions

- Utility bills: Electric (ABC Electric Company), Water (XYZ Water Works), Gas (GHI Gas Company)
- Internet and cable provider: Internet Provider XYZ, Cable Provider ABC
- Insurance premiums: XYZ Insurance Company
- Subscriptions: None

7. Other Relevant Information:

- Safe deposit box: Bank XYZ, Box No. 1234
- List of valuable assets: Jewelry, art, and collectibles stored in a secure location

- Outstanding legal issues or lawsuits: None

Remember to replace this generic information with your own personal details and specific accounts. It's essential to keep this information updated regularly and inform your loved ones or executor of its location and any changes.

II: Complete your "One-Page Will"

Fill in the following information to complete your "One-Page Will".

Family Name: ____________________

Address: ____________________

City: ____________ State: ________

Phone: ____________ Passcode: ________

Phone: ____________ Passcode: ________

Wife's name: ____________________

Date of Birth: ____________________

City of Birth: ________ State: ____ County: ________

Social Security number: ____________________

Wife's last year of education: ____________________

Wife's Parent's names

Mother: ____________________

Father: ____________________

Husband's name: ____________________

Date of Birth: ____________________

City of Birth: ________ State: ____ County: ________

Social Security number: ____________________

Husband's last year of education: ____________________

Husband's Parents names

Mother: ____________________

Father: ____________________

Where is your Marriage Certificate: ____________________

Child(ren): ______________________ DOB: ______________________

______________________ DOB: ______________________

WHERE ARE YOUR IMPORTANT PAPERS LOCATED?

Insurance policies, military documents, car titles, house deeds, apartment lease, bank statements, passwords, digital assets, birth certificates, Living Will, durable power of attorney, Will, Trust, etc.

____

____

____

NAMES, ADDRESSES AND PHONE NUMBERS OF PROFESSIONAL ADVISORS

Name of Clergy	Address	Phone
______________	______________	______________

Name of Doctors	Address	Phone
______________	______________	______________
______________	______________	______________
______________	______________	______________

Name of Attorney	Address	Phone
______________	______________	______________
______________	______________	______________

Name of Tax Preparer	Address	Phone
______________	______________	______________

Name of Insurance Agents	Address	Phone
______________	______________	______________
______________	______________	______________
______________	______________	______________

LIVING WILL

Who has a copy? (yours) ____________________ (spouse's) ________________

When was it updated? (yours) ____________________ (spouse's) _______________

DURABLE POWER OF ATTORNEY

Who has a copy? (yours) ____________________ (spouse's) ______________

When was it updated? (yours) ___________________ (spouse's) ______________

EXECUTOR(S) OF WILL

Name	Address	Phone
___________________________	______________________	_________________
___________________________	______________________	_________________

If you have a will, is your Will filed in Probate Court in your county? If so, where is your will filed?

State:_______________ County:_________________

TRUST

If you have set up a trust, it is important to mention it in your Will and outline how the assets held in the trust should be distributed.

____

____

____

____

____

BURIAL WISHES
DO NOT FORGET TO INCLUDE A PICTURE YOU WANT USED FOR YOUR OBITUARY.

Funeral Home Name: ____

Address: ____

Phone: ______________________ Email: ____________________________

Website: ____

Personal Burial Wishes (ex. Traditional burial or cremation, location, etc.)
Wife's wishes:

____

____

Husband's wishes:

____

____

Guardianship

Have you ever thought about who you would select or designate to act for you – if you are unable?

Long-term Guardian for Minor Children:

Name	Address	Phone
______________________	__________________	_____________
______________________	__________________	_____________

Short-Term Guardian for Minor Children:

If you have children under the age of 18, who would be available immediately to them (within 20 minutes) if you could not be located.

Name	Address	Phone
______________________	__________________	_____________
______________________	__________________	_____________

<u>Long or Short-term Guardian for Pet(s):</u>

If you have pets, who would be able to care for them immediately in your absence.

Name	Address	Phone
______________________	______________________	______________
______________________	______________________	______________

LIFE INSURANCE POLICIES AND ANNUITIES

<u>TYPE</u>: (Term, Whole Life, Group Life, Annuity.) Insurance company name, face amount (death benefit), whose life is insured, and who owns the policy.

Insurance policies (#____________) along with beneficiaries.

Wife
Insurance Company: ________________________________
Policy Numbers: ___________________________________
Beneficiaries
Primary: ____________________ Contingent: ____________________

Husband
Insurance Company: ________________________________
Policy Numbers: ___________________________________
Beneficiaries
Primary: ____________________ Contingent: ____________________

Child(ren)
Insurance Company: ________________________________
Policy Numbers: ___________________________________
Beneficiaries
Primary: ____________________ Contingent: ____________________

Child(ren)
Insurance Company: ________________________________
Policy Numbers: ___________________________________
Beneficiaries
Primary: ____________________ Contingent: ____________________

RETIREMENT PLANS

Type: Pension, Profit Sharing, IRA, SEP, 401k, 403B. Describe the type of plan, the plan name, the current value of the plan, and any other pertinent information.

INVESTMENTS

Acct #____________________ Contact: ____________________
Husband:
Company name: ________________________IRA Account: _______________

Beneficiaries
Primary: ____________________ Contingent: ____________________

Acct #____________________ Contact: ____________________

Wife
Company name: ________________________IRA Account: _______________

Beneficiaries
Primary: ____________________ Contingent: ____________________

STOCKS, CERTIFICATE OF DEPOSIT(S) AND BONDS

Husband
Company name: __________________________________

Stock(s) Account: ____

Beneficiaries
Primary: ____________________ Contingent: ____________________

Wife
Company name: __________________________________

Stock(s) Account: ____

Beneficiaries
Primary: ____________________ Contingent: ____________________

CRYPTOCURRENCY

Company name: ______________________________

Website: ______________________________

Username: ______________________ Password: ______________________

BANK AND SAVINGS ACCOUNTS [PAYABLE ON DEATH (POD)]

Type: Checking, Savings, Certificate of Deposit, and Money Market

Bank Name: ______________________________ (POD)

Address: ______________________________

Phone: ______________________ Email: ______________________

Website: ______________________________

Beneficiaries
Primary: ____________________ Contingent: ____________________

Bank Name: ______________________________ (POD)

Address: ______________________________

Phone: ______________________ Email: ______________________

Website: ______________________________

Beneficiaries
Primary: ____________________ Contingent: ____________________

CERTIFICATE OF DEPOSIT (CD)

Account Holder Name:
ROUTING #______________________ ACCOUNT #______________________

Beneficiaries
Primary: ____________________ Contingent: ____________________
Payable On Death (POD) ______________________________

SOCIAL SECURITY OFFICE

1 (800) 772-1213 and/or (TTY 1 (800) 325-0778; https://www.ssa.gov

TITLE TO CARS [TRANSFER ON DEATH (TOD)]

CAR 1: ____

CAR 2: ____

LIST ASSETS OR PERSONAL PROPERTY

List only your major personal effects such as, jewelry, collections, antiques, furs, and all other valuable non-business personal property (indicate type below and give a lump sum value for miscellaneous, less valuable items).

Description	Owner	Market Value

PASSWORDS

We all have passwords that we use everyday and should be mindful that along with other valuable assets someone should have access to your passwords to be able to access your accounts, computer, and phone upon your death.

Name Address Phone

______________________ ______________________ ______________

TAXES

It is advisable to make sure you have a person designated to file your taxes the year of your death.

Name Address Phone

______________________ ______________________ ______________

BUSINESS INTERESTS

Type: General and Limited Partnership, Sole Proprietorships, privately owned corporations, professional, farm, and ranch interests.
Give a description of the interests, who has the interest, your ownership in the interests, and the estimated value of the interests.

As a business owner, it is important for you to create an 'Exit Plan' in the event of your death. What happens to your business if you are incapacitated or upon your death?

Exit Plan:

MONTHLY BILLS AND SUBSCRIPTIONS

List monthly bills and subscriptions. It's important to include account numbers, due dates, and if these are on automatic withdrawal what account they are being withdrawn from as well.

Utility bills (electricity, water, gas):

Smartphone, Internet and cable providers:

Insurance premiums (health insurance, auto insurance, home insurance, or life insurance):

Subscriptions (anti-virus, streaming services, digital newspapers, magazine subscriptions, regular and streaming services like Netflix, Hulu, or Spotify, Microsoft, Apple etc.):

Credit Cards (American Express, Apple, Visa, Macys, etc.):

Debts Owed

Debts owed to you: If someone owes you money, you can specify how these debts should be handled or forgiven in your will:

Other Pertinent Information

INDEX

G

H

I

L

M

N

O

P

WORKS CITED

Asset | English meaning - Cambridge dictionary. (n.d.). https://dictionary.cambridge.org/dictionary/english/asset

Beneficiary | English meaning - Cambridge Dictionary. (n.d.). https://dictionary.cambridge.org/dictionary/english/beneficiary

Consumer Financial Protection Bureau. (2024, May 14). Revocable living trust. Consumer Financial Protection Bureau. http://www.consumerfinance.gov

File the final income tax returns of a deceased person. Internal Revenue Service. (n.d.). https://www.irs.gov/individuals/file-the-final-income-tax-returns-of-a-deceased-person

Fisher, Jennifer, Mms. (2023, December 12). 5 stages of grief: Coping with the loss of a loved one. Harvard Health. https://www.health.harvard.edu/mind-and-mood/5-stages-of-grief-coping-with-the-loss-of-a-loved-one

Hayes, A. (2024, March 19). Fiduciary definition: Examples and why they are important. Investopedia. https://www.investopedia.com/terms/f/fiduciary.asp

Hayes, A. (n.d.). Primary beneficiary: Explanation, importance and examples. Investopedia. https://www.investopedia.com/terms/p/primary-beneficiary.asp#:~:text=A%20primary%20beneficiary%20is%20an%20individual%20or%20organization,beneficiaries%20and%20stipulate%20how%20distributions%20would%20be%20allocated

Inheritance | definition in the Cambridge English dictionary. (n.d.-b). https://dictionary.cambridge.org/us/dictionary/english/inheritance

Kagan, J. (2024, July 31). Contingent beneficiary: Definition, characteristics, and benefits. Investopedia. https://www.investopedia.com/terms/c/contingent_beneficiary.asp

Kagan, J. (2024, August 31). Irrevocable trusts explained: How they work, types, and uses. Investopedia. https://www.investopedia.com/terms/i/irrevocabletrust.asp

Kagan, J. (2024, April 22). What is estate planning? Definition, meaning, and key components. Investopedia. https://www.investopedia.com/terms/e/estateplanning.asp

Legal Information Institute. (n.d.). Adjudication. Legal Information Institute. https://www.law.cornell.edu/wex/adjudication

Legal Information Institute. (2022b, June). Advance directive. Legal Information Institute. https://www.law.cornell.edu/wex/advance_directive

Legal Information Institute. (2021, November). Conservatorship. Legal Information Institute. https://www.law.cornell.edu/wex/conservatorship

Legal Information Institute. (2022, January). Guardianship. Legal Information Institute. https://www.law.cornell.edu/wex/guardianship

Legal Information Institute. (n.d.). Escheat. Legal Information Institute.
https://www.law.cornell.edu/wex/escheat

Legal Information Institute. (2020, December). Fiduciary relationship. Legal Information Institute.
https://www.law.cornell.edu/wex/fiduciary_relationship

Legal Information Institute. (2023, June). Living will. Legal Information Institute.
https://www.law.cornell.edu/wex/living_will

Legal Information Institute. (n.d.-c). Probate court. Legal Information Institute.
https://www.law.cornell.edu/wex/probate_court

Legal Information Institute. (2022, April). Term Life Insurance. Legal Information Institute.
https://www.law.cornell.edu/wex/term_life_insurance

Legal Information Institute. (2021, September). Transfer-on-death deed. Legal Information Institute.
https://www.law.cornell.edu/wex/transfer-on-death_deed

Legal Information Institute. (2024, July). Whole life insurance. Legal Information Institute.
https://www.law.cornell.edu/wex/whole_life_insurance

Legal Information Institute. (2022, April). Universal Life Insurance. Legal Information Institute.
https://www.law.cornell.edu/wex/universal_life_insurance

Liberty Mutual Insurance Company. (2024, September 30). Death Benefit. Liberty Mutual Insurance Company.
https://www.libertymutual.com/death benefit

Mayo Foundation for Medical Education and Research. (2022, August 2). Your guide to living wills and other advance directives. Mayo Clinic. https://www.mayoclinic.org/healthy-lifestyle/consumer-health/in-depth/living-wills/art-20046303#:~:text=Living%20will,pain%20management%20or%20organ%20donation.

MetLife Services and Solutions, LLC. (2024, September). Policyholder. MetLife Services and Solutions, LLC. https://www.metlife.com/stories/benefits/what-is-a-policyholder/

Ordp, O. (n.d.). Understanding Supplemental Security Income (SSI) SSI for children. Social Security Administration. https://www.ssa.gov/ssi/text-child-ussi.htm

Sheikh, Z. (Ed.). (2023, August 20). Five Stages of Grief. WebMD.com. https://www.webmd.com

Smith, M., Robinson, L., & Segal, J. (2024, October 23). Coping with Grief and Loss Stages of Grief, the Grieving Process, and Learning to Heal. HelpGuide.org. http://www.helpguide.org

Social Security. Disability Determination Process. (n.d.). Adjudication of disability. https://www.ssa.gov/disability/determination.htm

Social Security benefits and how to apply: Usagov. Social Security benefits and how to apply | USAGov. (n.d.). https://www.usa.gov/what-is-social-security

Social Security definition | Cambridge English dictionary. (n.d.-c). https://dictionary.cambridge.org/us/dictionary/english/social-security

The United States Social Security Administration: SSA. Social Security. (n.d.). https://www.ssa.gov

Tretina, K. (2024, September 13). What happens to Credit Card Debt When You Die? Yahoo! Finance. https://finance.yahoo.com/personal-finance/what-happens-to-credit-card-debt-when-you-die-195732443.html

Wikimedia Foundation. (2024, September 2). Death and taxes (idiom). Wikipedia. https://en.wikipedia.org/wiki/Death_and_taxes_(idiom)

ABOUT THE AUTHOR

Marchell G. Short has lived her life in dedication to helping people. She has advanced degrees from both the University of Cincinnati and Xavier University, Cincinnati, OH. She spent 30 years as an Urban High School Business-Technology and Special Education High School Teacher for Cincinnati Public Schools, Cincinnati, Ohio.

For the last forty plus years, Marchell has assisted thousands of families by owning and operating her own Income Tax Service, MGSHORT Income Tax Service. She later expanded her services by becoming a Dave Ramsey Certified Financial Peace University Coordinator and Financial Coach.

Through the Dave Ramsey Program, Marchell has assisted hundreds of families in their journey to becoming Debt-Free by conducting both in person and virtual classes. She is known as a 'Budgeting Guru'. If you're in debt, she can coach you into becoming debt-free in order to live your best life.

Marchell is retired and resides in Florida with her husband of 49 years, Howard. They are the proud parents of four adult children, grandparents of three lovely grandchildren and two bonus great-grandchildren.

As a minister's wife, Marchell along with Howard have had the privilege to assist 100's of families when facing loved ones at end of life with palliative care and estate planning.

Marchell has written this book from the heart of a teacher, with the aim of providing her guidance as you navigate the process of estate planning, particularly preparing your Last Will or creating the necessary documents to enable your executor to smoothly execute your final wishes.

WHERE THERE IS A WILL, THERE IS A WAY

ESTATE PLANNING MADE EASY FOR YOU

FOLLOW MARCHELL G. SHORT

LINKTR.EE/MGSHORTTAXSVC

@MGSHORTTAX

@MGSHORTINCOMETAXSVC

WWW.MGSHORTTAXSVC.COM

www.ingramcontent.com/pod-product-compliance
Lightning Source LLC
LaVergne TN
LVHW070854210926
848482LV00016B/930